Johnny Cash

He Walked the Line

1932–2003

Johnny Cash

He Walked the Line
1932–2003

GARTH
CAMPBELL

JOHN BLAKE

Published by John Blake Publishing Ltd,
3, Bramber Court, 2 Bramber Road,
London W14 9PB, England

www.blake.co.uk

First published in paperback in 2005

ISBN 1 84454 097 9

British Library Cataloguing-in-Publication Data:

A catalogue record for this book is available from the British Library.

Design by www.envydesign.co.uk

Printed in Great Britain by Bookmarque

1 3 5 7 9 10 8 6 4 2

Papers used by ??? Publishing are natural, recyclable products made from wood
grown in sustainable forests. The manufacturing processes conform to the
environmental regulations of the country of origin.

Every attempt has been made to contact the relevant copyright-holders,
but some were unobtainable. We would be grateful if the appropriate people
could contact us.

This book is dedicated to Johnny Cash.
His life provided the inspiration for so many born
on the wrong side of the tracks ...

Contents

Foreword

Johnny Cash, six feet two, 250 pounds and closely resembling an outlaw Indian, was a strong presence on any stage. His long black hair swept over a satin collar. His left eye, weakened from a childhood bout of measles, drooped a little when he was tired. His nose was crooked, the result of a car crash one rainy night which also cost him six front teeth. His mean, pockmarked face was clearly unused to smiling. There was a scar on his right cheek caused by the removal of a cyst, although it was later rumoured to be a bullethole. He always sang from the right side of his mouth – 'whopper-jawed', his beloved wife June Carter called it – the left side hung on his face purely for balance. His battle with the elements left him looking far older than his years. He resembled a card shark out of the Old West or a New Orleans rakehell on his way to duel over a woman. But the inner strength was omnipresent, from the lines on his face to the dents in his cheeks.

Cash was a country megastar who always told a story; he chronicled the hard times, the unhappy loves, the tragedies, the disasters, prison life, sharecropping, railroading, lumberjacking and cowpoking. His creative abilities transcended the labels of 'country' or 'western'. It's hard to define it, really. Yet here's a man who neither sang very well nor played the guitar impressively. He just did his best to get the tale told.

Johnny Cash sang about a world that's now more of a myth than reality, the world of those poor Southern whites from the Depression – closed, wary, brimming with gritty pride. That pain and suffering may no longer exist, but Cash's audiences pretty much always contained someone who'd never forgotten it.

Cash appealed to all generations. Perhaps it was because he always referred to a simpler America. And those audiences all knew how much he'd suffered personally; no wonder this haunted man survived the depths of drug addiction to sell more records and draw larger and wilder crowds than any other country singer in history.

Along the way there were some good times and many more bad ones. It wasn't until 1968, and the release of the album he recorded inside Folsom Prison, California, before a cheering audience of convicts, that Johnny Cash's name filtered into the non-rural corners of America. To convicts, hobos and no-hopers, Cash was a hero, even though he had little experience of prison himself. His songs of lost love, poverty, emotional homecomings and the Bible definitely hit the spot.

Jimmy Rogers may have been the father of country music (he died of tuberculosis in 1933 at the age of 35). The doomed, brilliant Hank Williams (dead at 29 after a life marred by use of drugs and alcohol) was undoubtedly its patron saint. But Johnny Cash was the uncrowned king. His life closely resembled that of Williams, but Cash managed – through a massive effort of will and thanks to the help of people who loved him – to triumph over his demons.

Cash was a multimillionaire thanks to vast record sales and lucrative concert appearances. He lived a luxurious lifestyle but never forgot his early suffering. Now that both he and his beloved wife June are no longer with us, he's left the memories of a rollercoaster life and the story of how one fine woman brought a man back from the brink on more than one occasion.

Johnny Cash always displayed the tendencies of a caged animal; constantly pacing up and down with nervous motion, his hands flitting like butterflies across his chest, shoulders and face, wiping away imaginary perspiration and tugging at his nose and ears. He was big and thick in the chest in the good old days, less raw-boned and gaunt than he had been when his life revolved around a nonstop diet of pills. The jet-black hair hung down over his collar back then and that trademark black frock coat and grey pinstriped trousers were there for all to see. By the time Johnny Cash came out of his drug-induced abyss in the late Sixties, his voice had taken on the tones of a nasal pipe organ with an Arkansas drawl. Cash decided that hard work was the only medicine that'd cure him of his drug addiction and that's what enabled him to overcome those demons in the end.

During the last twenty years or so of his life, Johnny Cash crossed the line to become the idol of a vast, popular mainstream audience. Tours through America involved luxurious buses, the superhighway, the limousine, the airport, the plane, the motel, the auditorium. At times it must have seemed as though he stood still while the backdrop raced behind him. Cash's personality, his talent, his social conscience and memory were ingrained in his growling, rusty-nail voice, which was as deep as an open wound, but could instantly convey another, older, America to any audience. At best his voice was something like smooth and mellow thunder. Earth-deep, occasionally ominous, resonant, virile, untrained and unconventional. It could also be lonely and haunting one minute and boomingly happy the next.

'He'd constantly bend the tone,' explained one music expert. 'He sang what was inside him, searching in a bewitching way for a note that wasn't always there. He decorated his melody according to his own interpretation. Some of his songs were akin to the old field cries of the Southern slaves, some were scattered with bass talk. They were bawdy, swinging poems.'

Johnny Cash was an original – perhaps the roughest diamond of all. But a diamond all the same.

1

J R CASH

Scottish mariner William Cash arrived in Westmoreland County, Virginia, in 1673, to find a land so bleak and winds-wept it seemed almost identical to the Scottish Highlands he'd just left behind.

The Cash family didn't stay long and had soon moved to Amherst and Bedford Counties to work as planters and soldiers while the American Revolution took shape. In 1810, William Cash's grandson Moses was an early settler in Henry County, Georgia. The family property was virtually destroyed during the Civil War, though the ruins of that building remain standing to this day.

The appalling burning of Atlanta and the destruction of plantations throughout Georgia forced Moses Cash's son Reuban to escape the war by heading for Arkansas in an ox-drawn wagon with his young family. They eventually settled in a town called Ribson, where Reuban named his newborn son William Henry Cash – after his great-grandfather William and Henry County. Reuban took up farming, raising everything that his family could eat.

William Henry Cash eventually became a Baptist minister, married Rebecca – a Baptist missionary – and had twelve children (four of whom died in infancy). Youngest child Ray was born on May 13, 1897, in Cleveland County, Arkansas. Two of his mother's brothers were also Baptist preachers. Ray Cash had a typical country boy upbringing in the rolling hills of Arkansas, beginning school at six and quitting at fourteen. He lost his father and mother while still in his teens.

On July 1, 1916, Ray Cash enlisted in the US Army to fight in World War I. Years later, Ray would sit his sons Johnny and Jack and their sister Reba on his knee and tell them stories about his exploits in France. But Ray never revealed the truth about the ugly scenes of death and destruction he had witnessed. Instead, he'd sing the children songs such as 'Over There' or one about an army mule called 'Simon Slicker'.

Ray wasn't the greatest of soldiers. In 1918, he was performing convoy duties out of the French town of St Lazare and was ordered to escort a trainload of beef to Paris. As it turned out, Ray encountered a pretty French girl and didn't turn up in time to ride with the train. Fortunately, it still arrived at its rightful destination. Ray even got a free trip to bohemian Paris, plus a promise from his commanding officer that he'd not be reported for neglecting his duties. In 1919 Ray got himself discharged at Fort Roote, Texas, and returned to his family in Arkansas. On arrival back in

Cleveland County, he proudly showed off his papers, which described him as having been 'an excellent soldier', despite his involvement in a number of disastrous mishaps.

Ray and his brother Jack soon got jobs cutting oak and cypress trees for a new bridge being built across the Saline River, near Kingsland, Arkansas. It was tough work, with nonstop physical exertion and long hours. Lunch breaks were just fifteen minutes and there was barely time to even chat with his workmates. But Ray knew he was a lucky man – many other ex-servicemen in the area had come back to nothing.

A few weeks of dawn-to-dusk slogging on that bridge followed. Then, one day, Ray spotted a pretty girl smiling at him from across the river. He got back to his work in case his foreman spotted him, but every time he looked up she was still there. Eventually she walked close enough to tell him her name was Carrie. Ray arranged to meet her at the town café later that day – and then told her to scram before he got into trouble. That evening, Carrie asked Ray and his brother back to her family home, where her parents gave the boys their first proper meal in weeks. They also offered the Cash brothers board and lodging at their home for a dollar a day. Ray noticed the sparkle in Carrie's eyes when her parents made their generous offer to him and his brother. That was the moment he decided she was going to be his wife.

On August 18, 1920, Ray married Carrie after winning her parents' approval through his commitment to hard work and a regular wage. Ray soon became known in Kingsland, Arkansas, as a modest, quiet-living husband. The Cash legend has always given the impression the family were on the breadline; in fact, Ray Cash worked every day of his life

3

and single-handedly provided for his family. They were undoubtedly short of cash, but never a day went by when Ray Cash was not supporting his brood.

When the Depression hit in 1929, Ray Cash was one of the few men in Cleveland County, Arkansas, who still managed to work. He'd cut pulpwood, work at sawmills and even had a stint on the railroad. His pride and determination was an example to the rest of the family. His motto was simple: he would do any work in order to make sure there was a meal on the table at the end of each day.

Aside from Ray, the other big influence in the Cash household was God. Thanks was given to the Lord every mealtime for giving the Cash family the opportunity to eat. Johnny Cash would later recall that this prayer was a humble offering of gratitude because they really *were* thankful for their continued survival and good health.

Ray Cash also raised food and livestock on his land, which helped feed the family and some of their more needy neighbours. 'We never turned anyone away,' Ray proudly recalled many years later. The door was always open at the Cash household, even though there was an ever-growing family inside the house, now comprising oldest son Roy, Jack and Louise. Mother Carrie was still looking forward to having at least another three or four children, if that was God's will.

On February 26, 1932, Johnny Cash was born in Kingsland. His given name was simply J R Cash. He would use the name John only subsequently, after a stint in the service. 'Johnny' came even later, at the suggestion of Sam Phillips of Sun Records.

J R came into the world just as the Great Depression was raging through the country, destroying families, jobs and lives. Kingsland – once a prosperous cotton town – was falling apart as cotton prices reached an all-time low. Many families were forced to move to the cheaper countryside, where they could live off the land. Ray still managed to get work, but knew he had to travel to where the jobs were, which meant the family moving with him. Initially, they headed for nearby Fordyce and then on to a shack of a house in Saline. It had only wooden slats to cover the windows.

Ray worked six days a week, twelve hours a day, for a meagre twenty-five to fifty cents a day. Often, he'd hop on the freight trains to find new jobs, going as far as Memphis to the north and Charleston to the south. He would live on coffee and dry bread and send his earnings home to his family. In some towns, labourers such as Ray were warned never to leave their boarding rooms – the locals threatened to kill them for taking their work away. It was a dog-eat-dog existence.

One time, Ray got arrested by railroad police for 'riding the blinds' (travelling in the area between the baggage car and mail car of a freight train). He begged the cop not to charge him because he wanted to get home to his young family. Unexpectedly, it worked: he was let off with a warning and headed home to Carrie and the children.

By late 1934, word got around the Saline area of Arkansas that the Roosevelt administration was setting up a community for five hundred farmers of 'good character' who had suffered badly in the Depression. The Federal Emergency Relief Administration aimed to relocate the most deserving of landless families through what became 46 experimental resettlement projects throughout the country. The first was to be in Mississippi County, in north-east Arkansas, where the government had purchased sixteen thousand acres of uncleared swampland for six dollars an acre. Ray was soon patiently waiting in line to apply for government aid as part of the new commune. He was desperate to end the years of job hopping and determined to have his beloved family by his side. After answering questions about his family, birthplace and education, Ray filled out the forms and went home to wait. He'd already been warned his chances were slim.

But someone in the town put in a good word for Ray; his reputation as a go-getter had impressed the government sponsors. He was accepted with one condition: the Cashes had just 24 hours to pack up and move to Mississippi County. Ray later discovered he and his family were one of only five families initially chosen.

On March 23, 1935, Ray Cash hired a ton-and-a-half pick-up truck and they hauled their sparse belongings to Mississippi County. The cost of the vehicle and driver was tacked on to the cost of their new homestead. Up front in the cab, Carrie Cash held baby Reba and hugged Louise alongside the driver. Ray, Roy, Jack and three-year-old J R were huddled under a tarpaulin on the flatbed.

The 250-mile trip along muddy roads was cold and wet. A stinging rain froze on the windscreen as the truck lurched and slid from one mudhole to the next. One of Johnny Cash's earliest memories was of peering out the back and seeing icicles cracking off the swaying trees as they headed north. The flat black delta land of Mississippi County seemed bleak after the lush rolling meadows of the Cashes' previous home county. But the family's brand-new, five-bedroom white clapboard house at the end of a gravel road more than made up for it. Their new home, two-and-a-half miles from Dyess, Arkansas, was a palace in comparison to what they were used to. On their arrival, the Cash children looked up at the house in awe, though they soon concluded this was where they really belonged.

Finances were very tight. The Cash family were grateful to get beans twice a week and bread and gravy for breakfast, though Carrie always ensured huge portions were on offer. But there were problems right from the start. When Carrie stoked up the wood stove that very first day, the beans she was cooking turned green because the water was iron-hard. When she tried to cook tea it turned black as ink. Soup curdled like buttermilk. Ray fetched a few barrels and ten-pound bags of lime from the colony centre and put the barrels below the eaves to catch soft rainwater. The children were taught to fill a third of a fifty-gallon barrel from the well pump and slack the water with a cup of lime. The iron would settle with the lime to the sides and the bottom, and every week one of the children scraped away the hard green ring of sediment that had built up inside the barrel. The resulting water was soft enough for cooking and washing.

Ray built himself a mule-drawn sled on which to get in and out of town, but the runners constantly wore down on the rough roads. Eventually, he made a cart from the building lumber left over from the construction of the house. Then he found two old iron wheels and fastened them under the cart. The mule was kept with a part-Jersey milk cow and some

Poland China pigs in the barn. The Cashes also bought a large flock of laying hens.

Years later, Johnny acknowledged that the colony at Dyess was definitely moulded along socialist lines. And many landowners saw the new colony as a threat to the sharecropper tradition that underpinned the South's agricultural economy. Dyess's roots were more along the lines of Scandinavia than anything in Arkansas. One thing helped to ensure the survival of the Dyess Colony in the racially divided South of the 1930s: although Mississippi County was 40 per cent black, the colony was for whites only. The subject of skin colour was rarely ever referred to in Dyess; for the inhabitants, it wasn't a problem because it never arose.

People earned extra income by growing their own food and trading much of it at the cooperative store in the town. Ten pounds of sugar was worth 55 cents, a quart of peanut butter 25 cents, 48 pounds of flour $1.85. Men's handmade shirts went for 75 cents and even dressy Tom Sawyer-type suits sold for $1.25. At the Dyess Cafe, a fancy Sunday chicken dinner for two was just 75 cents.

'I remember riding to town in our two-wheeler cart,' Johnny Cash recalled many years later. 'We'd go to the store on Saturday. We had a shopping list – flour, tobacco, sugar, salt, coal, oil, matches. I could get a nickel's worth of candy. The counter was on the right, and the sugar and stick candy were in big glass jars, but the man that ran the store would always give us more than a nickel's worth.'

Young J R wore denim dungarees most of the time, although he did get himself a Tom Sawyer suit. He loved walking through the clothing section of the main store, gazing at all the fancy clothes and dreaming about one day being able to wear some of them. The Cashes attended a Baptist church, which was an old converted schoolhouse located on Road 15. (All the roads in the commune were numbered – sixteen in all; the Cash family lived on Road 3.) Church, God and religion played an even bigger role in the Cashes' life from the time they settled in Dyess. Young J R hated the actual church services but adored the songs, which made a lasting impression on him from a very young age. Johnny later recalled: 'The one thing that I remember most was the fear I felt in church. I didn't understand it as worship then. I only knew it was some place that Mama was making me go with her. The preacher terrified me. He shouted and cried and gasped. The longer he preached, the louder he got and the more he gasped for breath.'

Little J R was also confused about their choice of church, as hitherto his mother had been a Methodist. She told her children she loved the atmosphere of the Baptist church, which was why she insisted on them all attending. People in that church were completely caught up by the fever of the occasion with the preacher walking amongst the congregation pulling people out of their seats, shouting, 'Come to God! Repent!' Then he'd lead them to the altar, where they'd fall to their knees. Five-year-old Johnny Cash's knuckles often turned white as he held on tightly to the seat in front of him, nervously observing the proceedings. But every kind of musical instrument was allowed in the Church of God and Johnny never forgot the guitars, mandolins and banjos that accompanied the singing.

In 1937, Connie persuaded Ray to get a battery radio, and

Johnny began listening to those same church songs on the wireless. As a special treat during the week, the entire Cash clan would gather round the radio and listen to country music programmes such as *The Grand Ole Opry* and *Supper Time Frolics*. The family listened to WLW, Cincinnati; WJJD, Chicago; WSM, Nashville and a host of other stations. Cash later said he actually believed the songs he was listening to were being played especially for him. He'd sit and listen to the programmes until long after everyone had left the big, long wooden table where they would all sit. As J R listened, he'd carve in the table over and over with his knife. Initials and little chunks, little V-shaped cuts. He ended up ruining his mother's table, but she never complained.

The music the young J R heard was a development of the Kentucky and Tennessee folk songs that had become popular in the early part of the century. Much of this sound came from the rural areas where railroads tracked into once-isolated communities and mining towns sprouted up in the middle of farmland. There were even a few pianos in farm parlours, where folk would play sheet-music arrangements of these new songs. Locally adapted versions of these songs began to emerge with new syncopations and sophisticated rhythms, and out of those 'hillbilly' or 'country' music soon developed.

● ● ● ●

Despite working a six-day week, Ray Cash still managed to find time for his children and involved them in numerous activities around the house and in the surrounding fields. One of little J R's favourite chores was lathering up his daddy's face with shaving cream and then watching in fascination as Daddy Cash scraped his chin clean of stubble with a cut-throat razor.

Ray Cash had a nickname for everyone in his family. J R was known as 'Shoo-Doo' and continued to be called by that name for the following fifty or so years, although no one has ever worked out where the sobriquet came from. 'It was just kinda passed down from a few generations back,' explained a laidback Johnny years later.

Naturally, growing up in the countryside brought with it plenty of adventures to keep the kids amused. One time Ray Cash decided to sleep the night in the chicken house to stop a wildcat raiding the pen in darkness. That evening, Carrie and the kids were woken up by a shotgun blast at around midnight. J R, five at the time, woke bolt upright along with his younger sister Reba, three, and Jack, seven. Mama Cash grabbed a kerosene light and they all ran towards the back porch, where they found Ray Cash dragging one very dead wildcat behind him.

'He won't eat any more of our chickens,' proclaimed Daddy Cash proudly. Young Johnny looked down at the big cat with his sharp teeth still grinning and a shiver went up his spine. The animal weighed in at 27 pounds on a cotton scale as the Cash children crowded round and gawped at it.

Ray's encounter with the wildcat was soon the talk of the countryside around Dyess. Neighbours would pop round to the Cash house where Reba, Jack and J R all sprawled on the hide of that big wildcat, still grinning from the wooden floor of the porch. A fast-talking salesman from the *Dallas Star* eventually persuaded Carrie to trade the pelt for a year's free subscription to his newspaper, despite Ray's objections. That dead cat represented Johnny Cash's first encounter with minor celebrity and he later said he loved every minute of the experience.

Another very different memory of childhood for young J R was the never-ending daily work duties every member of the family faced. Ray Cash believed his children should know that hard work was good for them, and he needed all the help he could muster to support his vast family. By the age of four, Johnny was carrying gallon cans of water to his older brothers and sister in the nearby cotton fields. By the age of ten, he was working on the fields himself, as well as tending the garden corn and vegetable crops. All the kids were also expected to water and feed the animals, including the two plough mules, a cow and at least half a dozen pigs.

As Johnny Cash recalled many years later: 'We didn't get paid any money for choppin' or ploughin', but Daddy always paid us for picking cotton.' When asked in Dyess how long a day's work was, the reply was always the same: 'From the time you can see until the time you can't.'

There was another side to J R that put him on a different plain from his brothers and sisters: his tendency to daydream endlessly. The youngster had a vivid imagination and would spend hours gazing into the distance conjuring up magical thoughts about the world outside Arkansas. Something deep inside him said there was another life way beyond the county line. He was too young to know what that was, but it made him feel unsettled, even though he knew he was part of a loving, stable family.

Johnny's younger sister Reba later recalled: 'Daddy was

always having to tell J R to get to work because he was staring off at a bird or airplane or just leaning on his hoe. He was that kind of kid.'

Dyess was a sleepy little place. The centre of town consisted of Road 1 running east and west out of town, flanked by a general store, a service station, the Dyess Cafe and eventually a movie theatre where films starring the likes of Hollywood star Gene Autry would pack in the crowds on Saturday afternoons and evenings. The community was centred around the cannery, where people brought their produce or truck crops. The cannery took whatever was offered, cooked it, canned it and then gave back eight out of ten cans. They'd hold back the other two to help finance the place. If there was any extra money at the end of the year, the farmers were handed that back as well.

An incident at the bank in Dyess came to hold a significant place in Cash family folklore. One morning, J R's brother Roy, then aged fifteen, and a friend managed to wrest away a .32 revolver from a teenager who intended to hold up the bank and use the loot to run away from Dyess. (The bank subsequently burned down in 1936 and nobody ever saw fit to build a replacement.)

Over in Nashville, Tennessee, *The Grand Ole Opry* radio broadcast each and every week was going from strength to strength. Initially, the show's emphasis had been on instrumental music played by groups with bizarre names such as 'The Possum Hunters', 'The Gully Jumpers', 'The Snapper Whippers' and 'The Fruit Jar Drinkers'. After a while, the programme's 'old-timey' music catalogue was considered large enough to warrant its own section and was titled 'hillbilly'. Soon, artists such as Vernon Dalhart, Buell Kazee and The Carter Family were bringing this very special brand of music countrywide recognition.

Little Johnny Cash absorbed every second of it, listening closely to the radio in his family's living room and dreaming of how he might one day get himself on the music bandwagon.

2

BROTHER JACK

The weather in Mississippi County could be brutal sometimes. Summers were bone dry while winters often saw upwards of ten inches of snow in one storm. But the torrential downpour of rain that marked the opening month of 1937 was worse than anything ever seen before. It bucketed down for 21 days and nights. J R, then just short of his fifth birthday, and his family spent their days watching helplessly from the living-room window as the water in the front yard rose until it swept under their porch.

Inside the house, the Cashes listened intently to the family radio; the news reported that the Mississippi River was up to forty-nine feet – fifteen feet *above* flood level. As Johnny recalled years later: 'The Mississippi was full and didn't have no place to go, then she froze over. When the Mississippi gets full, she's dangerous, I'll tell you.' There were genuine fears that, if the river levees broke, the Dyess Colony where J R and his family lived would literally be swept away. Then they heard the Tennessee River had also flooded and strong winds were battering the levees into a state of near collapse. Ray Cash gathered his young family into the front room of the house and told them they should grab a few belongings and leave immediately. He'd stay behind with oldest son Roy, then thirteen, and try to save the house. Carrie and the children didn't want to go any place without Ray, but he insisted they needed to move – fast.

Carrie decided to head with the children for Kingsland, where she had family. At the nearest railroad station, the family boarded a train that took ten agonising hours to cover one hundred miles because of fallen logs on the tracks and the ever-present danger of flooding. Despite his young age at the time, Johnny never forgot that epic journey. 'It was late at night, and everybody on the train was sleeping. My mother, I remember, had dressed me in my new suit. I kept running up and down the aisles. Down near Stuttgart, Arkansas, we weren't moving more than five miles an hour because the water was clear over the tracks. I remember a lot of the women and children crying because they were so worried and upset.'

Back at the farm, Ray and Roy jammed the front and back doors of the house open so the water would pass through the property, hopefully taking the mud with it. They brought the chickens in from the henhouse and stuck them in the living room. The family dog, a large brown rabbit hound, was left in the hallway to protect the other animals. Ray Cash, not knowing when – if ever – he'd be back, grabbed a precious fifty-pound ham from the kitchen and cut it into chunks on the floor for the dog.

On January 24, 1937, Ray and Roy dragged the cow and mule from the barn and, with a last glance back at their home, retreated to the safety of the higher ground where they watched and prayed as the waters surged across the fields. Boatloads of armed deputies floated around on boats to prevent looting of the colonies. Father and son sloshed two-and-a-quarter miles to the main mule barn in Dyess, which was doubling up as a rescue centre. Ray and Roy didn't reach their family in Kingsland until a week later.

When the floods finally subsided more than a month later, the Cash family returned to the house to find it in ruins. Packs of dogs were running wild, cottonmouth moccasins and rattlesnakes had gone to the high ground and were living in several outhouses. Chickens had laid eggs throughout the house, which the children carefully collected and stored in the kitchen. The broody sow in the barn had somehow given birth to 'five of the prettiest spotted Poland China pigs you ever saw', Johnny Cash later recalled. Miraculously, they all survived.

Ray Cash and his family were luckier than most. Despite mud saturating the floors – up to one foot in places – the house was standing and most of the livestock had been saved. And the flood waters had even left the soil richer than before, which provided the Cashes with their best ever cotton crop the following year. Out of all that misery something good had grown. It taught J R that out of all the unhappiness in the world could spring some hope.

On February 5, 1938, Ray Cash was offered outright

ownership of his twenty-acre farm. The property had originally been valued at $2,684.90, but he'd put so much work into it – including completely clearing and planting the land – that the purchase price was dropped to $2,183.60. It was still a lot of money for a poor Arkansas farmer to find but, once converted into a mortgage he could pay off at $111.41 – or 6 per cent – a year, it was too good an opportunity to miss. The Cashes went on to plant, chop and harvest eighteen crops on their Dyess farm.

Within a year of the flood of '37 the colony had grown to 637 homesteads with a post office and a drug store in Dyess plus the movie theatre, which was by now the social mecca of the town. Trouble in Dyess was pretty rare. About the best-remembered incident following the great flood was when two bums matching half dollars on the cafe porch one rainy day exchanged some heated words. One went for his jackknife; the other began hitting him so hard and fast that he never got it open. Sheriff's deputies broke up the fight before anyone was seriously hurt. Troublemakers were asked to leave the colony before they caused any real problems. Industriousness, thrift, honesty and religious zeal flourished so strongly in Dyess that it was inevitable young J R would eventually start to feel frustrated by the environment, a resentment that would erupt into rebellion years later.

The locals always had fond memories of the Cashes, especially father Ray. 'They were accommodating, nice neighbours,' gas station owner Frank Huff later recalled. 'They'd help you in any way they could. Old man Cash – he was kinda highly strung, but he was a hustler. He was a worker.' And Ray's 'hustling' certainly rubbed off on his boys, all of whom were taught the importance of 'getting out there and making a name for themselves' from an early age.

Almost thirty years later, Johnny Cash brought a movie documentary crew to Dyess and they shot a lot of film footage of old Frank Huff at his filling station. But Huff remained unaffected by the celebrity status bestowed upon him by the documentary. 'Some folk from California came through here and asked for my autograph, but I was working,' he said afterwards.

• • • •

Truth be told, back in the late 1930s little J R Cash was not really a very notable child. His mother Carrie once said of her son, 'He was the quietest one of the children. Hardly ever said anythin'. But he listened. He was drinkin' it all in.' And there lay the key to Johnny's childhood. He liked to watch things from a distance, storing up the memories so that he could dip into the fragments of his own mind years later, when millions would listen to his every word.

J R's only vice at this time was that he loved smoking grapevine when he was out on the cotton fields. It didn't matter that it made him cough, he still liked to inhale the putrid smoke of those burning leaves – and he started when he was only about eight years old. This addiction would eventually develop into something that would threaten the very fabric of his life.

In 1938, Johnny's baby sister Joann was born, followed in 1940 by kid brother Tommy. Seven hungry mouths were a lot for Ray Cash to feed. When eldest son Roy graduated from

Dyess High School in 1939, he had to pick strawberries from the family patch and then hawk them at the colony centre to afford to buy a grey graduation suit that cost a whopping $15.98. Shortly after his graduation, Roy married sweetheart Wandene Pickens and moved more than forty miles north to Blytheville, where he found a job on a dragline for $25 a week – good wages at the time.

Meanwhile, the other six children went off to school in Dyess on the school bus – a converted truck with a canvas top. Carrie Cash turned out the lunches in bulk and each child carried a paper sack with a meat sandwich, a hunk of home-made cheese and some newly baked doughnuts or cookies. Eventually the school offered fifteen-cent lunches, but that would have cost the Cashes up to ninety cents a day, so the children either stuck to packed lunches or got new jobs in the cafeteria to earn the meal.

Young J R had a dog, which he named Jake after one of the Dyess town supervisors who used to call round the house for a coffee and a piece of home-made apple pie. But one day while J R was at school, the dog broke into the hen coop. When Ray Cash found him, the dog had already slaughtered half a dozen chickens and was attacking another. Enraged, Ray fetched his gun and shot the dog. A short time later, J R came home from school, immediately sensed something had happened to his pooch and followed its trail into the woods, where he found the dog's corpse. Rushing back to the house in floods of tears, he kept asking his father, 'Why? Why? Why?' Ray Cash told his son the truth and J R walked away heartbroken but never again mentioned the incident to his father. Ray later bitterly regretted killing the dog and admitted that day haunted him for many years: 'I wouldn't have killed that dog if I'd thought about it. I dragged the dog back into the woods. I hated the killing, but it was done.'

All those years on the farm in Dyess helped seal an unbreakable bond of friendship between J R and his older brother, Jack, even though they were completely opposite characters in many ways. Jack was a relaxed, laidback boy while his younger brother was known to everyone as a nervous bundle of energy who frequently retreated into himself and said little or nothing to anyone. And some of the boys' adventures together got them into a heaonful of trouble. One time, Ray Cash went out looking for a missing chicken and found the two boys in a little wood shack frying the animal up in a skillet over an open fire. The boys made no attempt to deny what had happened – such was the value of the term 'honesty' in the Cash household that neither of them was ever recalled lying, 'even if they knew they were going to get a whippin' for what they had done,' said Ray years later.

J R, a thin, bony kid, looked up to Jack, a husky 143 pounds when he was only fourteen. The older boy had toned his muscles through hours of working with a set of weights he had built himself in the barn and a Charles Atlas course on body building he'd sent off for when he turned thirteen.

While J R was more often than not to be found listening enthusiastically to the radio, Jack became attached to the Bible. So much so that he talked openly at the local church about his ambition to become a preacher when he grew up. Jack took his bible everywhere he went – to school, to work, to church – and studied it by the hour.

The Cash house had no electricity, so Jack would sit and

read the Bible at the kitchen table with a kerosene lamp, keeping one ear open to all that music on the radio. As did his younger brother: 'I'd turn it down a little and get my ear closer in. I had to hear those songs. Nothing in the world was as important to me as hearing those songs on that radio. The music carried me up above the mud, the work and the hot sun,' Johnny later recalled.

J R and Jack often walked to the co-op store in Dyess to get groceries for the family. The store had been taken over by a stern-faced man called Mr Steele, a member of a sect that claimed they were the only truly divine members on the earth. Jack tried to avoid all conversation with Mr Steele on the basis that he didn't want to end up arguing with him. It wasn't always possible, though. One hot summer's day, when Johnny and Jack walked into the store, Mr Steele suddenly rounded on Jack – who always walked round town with his bible in his hand – and said, 'Jack, you know if you don't belong to my church you're going to hell, don't you?'

There was a long beat of silence. Then Jack looked directly at Mr Steele, smiled and began singing:

> Have you been to Jesus for the cleansing power,
> Are you washed in the blood of the Lamb?
> Are you fully trusting in His grace this hour,
> Are you washed in the blood of the Lamb?

Mr Steele's face turned red. He picked up a knife he'd been chopping meat with and stabbed the counter in front of him before storming off. The two Cash boys walked out without a word passing between them.

Jack was the Dyess paperboy and J R often watched him loading his papers, mostly *Memphis Press-Scimitar*s, in his bicycle basket and delivering them to every home in the community. No matter what the weather was like, Jack saw it as his personal responsibility to deliver those papers. He also knew the family needed his contribution to the weekly grocery bill.

Jack was particularly protective towards J R because his kid brother was the skinny, weak one in the family. 'There was nobody in the world as good and as wise and as strong as my big brother Jack,' Johnny would say proudly. Jack also handed down sensible advice on schoolwork and the issues of the day. In many ways he was another father figure to J R.

• • • •

May 12, 1944, was a beautiful warm Saturday morning in Arkansas. The lush black dirt was growing good cotton to be hoed, ploughed and picked, and the Cash family were even selling a few watermelons out by the mailbox in front of the farm.

Jack Cash was due to go to work at the school workshop that day and J R was planning a fishing trip to one of the larger drainage ditches that ran through Dyess. Well, they called them 'ditches', but they were really more like small rivers.

J R was desperate for his big brother to go with him, but Jack felt obliged to contribute towards the family's struggle for survival. The three dollars he'd pick up for a Saturday at the workshop cutting fence posts and cleaning up the bushes and weeds around the agriculture shop was essential to the Cash weekly income.

'Why don't you come fishin' with me?' J R pleaded with his older brother.

'I gotta work today 'cause that three dollars will help a lot,' answered Jack, as he stood in the middle of the living-room floor with his hands on a kitchen chair that he spun around and around. It was a stunt that always transfixed J R.

Jack clearly didn't feel like working that day, but those family obligations were resting heavily on his shoulders. He even admitted to his kid brother, 'I just don't feel like I should work today but I gotta.' When mother Carrie heard Jack's remark she told him not to go to work if he felt like that. Jack insisted, although, significantly, he stalled his departure for a few more minutes by impersonating Bugs Bunny to make his kid brother laugh. Finally, the two boys set out from the house together. J R reluctantly left his brother to go off fishing when they reached a fork in the track. Jack was still kidding around and making faces at J R as he walked off in the distance.

J R didn't get one bite that day. About noon, he set off home from the ditch with his fishing pole over his shoulder once more. When he reached the spot where he'd left his brother not two hours earlier, he noticed the town preacher and Ray Cash in an A-model Ford coming straight towards him. The moment he saw his father's face he knew something was wrong.

'We got home and Daddy took me to the smokehouse. He had a paper sack under his arm. He took out Jack's clothes and showed me the blood on the ripped shirt and trousers. "You can see how bad he's been hurt," he told me. "I'm afraid we're gonna lose him." It was the first and only time I ever saw my daddy cry,' Johnny later recalled.

Jack Cash had been cutting fenceposts behind the workshop when he reached for the handle of the circular saw. The saw jerked him into the moving sawblade and he fell on to it. An ambulance driver reported that, when he found Jack, he was holding his own stomach and told the driver calmly, 'I picked up as much of my intestines as I could, but there was about six feet of it that got chopped up.' He then said to the driver, 'Tell me something happy, 'cause I'm gonna die.'

Jack was taken to the small hospital in Dyess, where he lived for a further eleven days. J R's three younger siblings at the time – Joann, Tommy and Reba – were taken to stay at a neighbour's house while the rest of the family slept on makeshift beds at the hospital. J R saw his brother conscious on two occasions before he died. The first time was when he walked into the hospital room to find Jack just managing to talk to his mother. He didn't even look up when his younger brother came into the room. In fact, he would not (or perhaps could not) acknowledge J R's presence. The second time J R saw his brother was when he walked in and found him reading a letter from the girl he was dating and had wanted to marry. Once again, the two brothers said nothing to each other.

Years later, Johnny put his own interpretation on why his brother never spoke to him from his death bed. 'It was like he was saying by *not* talking to me, "There's no need telling you about what's going to happen because you know I'm going. Any time now, you're going to learn to live without me, so start learning now."'

Shortly after that second visit of J R's, doctors told the

Cashes that Jack had gangrene and warned that he could die at any moment. The family gathered around his bed. Naturally, there was a lot of crying and a lot of praying. Jack then fell into a coma. At about midnight he started hallucinating and talking to his father, Ray. He mentioned the crops and the fields of cotton and that they had to get the weeds out of the cotton. 'If it keeps on raining, we won't get back to the fields, Daddy. We must get the crabgrass out if we're gonna raise any cotton this year, if we're gonna have anything this winter.'

At 6:00am the next morning, skinny little J R was woken up by the sound of someone praying as he lay asleep in the room next to his brother. It was Ray Cash, who had sensed the time had come for his son to die. J R and his father moved next door to Jack's room and waited their turn to say farewell. J R bent over his brother's bed and put his cheek against Jack and said, 'Goodbye, Jack.'

A few moments later, Jack regained consciousness and squeezed his mother's hand before crying, 'And the angels are singing. Oh, Mama, I wish you could hear the angels singing!' Those were his last words.

Jack Cash died on May 21, 1944. His body was brought home to rest in the living room of the Cash family home for the Monday and Tuesday before the funeral. Townsfolk swarmed by – overflowing into the yard at times – to pay their respects, and people kneeled by the casket.

At Jack's funeral, six boy scouts carried his coffin. As J R watched the coffin being laid to rest, he wobbled on his own two feet he felt so heartbroken. Over Jack's grave at the north end of the cemetery, a modest polished granite headstone was mounted, reading: *Jack D. Cash 1929–1944*. At the top was the boy scout crest, and below it the question that Johnny Cash would carry with him for the rest of his life: 'Will You Meet Me In Heaven?'

One of J R's former teachers, Miss Kay Williams, was so worried about the effect his brother's death had had on the younger boy that she wrote him a moving note from her home in Longview, Texas.

> *Dearest J.R.*
> *Mrs Holland has already written to me about poor Jack. Honey, I can't tell you how much it grieved me to hear about it. Jack was such a sweet, nice boy and I know that no one can take his place, but we know he is at rest with Jesus ...*

J R was now the oldest son on the family farm. But he'd paid a high price for that title. The shock of losing his brother made him withdraw into himself even further than before. 'He became less peaceful. He thought more and talked even less,' recalled his sister Reba. Initially, J R couldn't get Jack out of his mind. Every thought was shared with Jack; every movement needed his approval.

At the Cash home, grief filled every room. Carrie Cash found Jack's cracker tin of savings; without counting it, she gave the money over to the Baptist church, but tucked the tin away for herself. Meanwhile, the first cotton had broken through the ground. Weeds had been let flourish far too long. Ray Cash, older and greyer after watching his son's dying days, had to put his overalls on once more and work his slow way down the new rows of cotton, chopping at the weeds with a worn hoe. Life had to go on.

A few days after the funeral, J R ambled across a field, looked out at a little bayou and right in the middle of that bayou was the tallest cypress tree for miles around. It stood all alone. The tree itself was dead, but the trunk still stood strong and tall. At the top of the tree the limbs were broken, twisted and gnarled by some past summer storm. Johnny remembered how Jack and he had often climbed that tree and swung from its vines. After walking on, he reached a sandy rise where he, his father and Jack used to plant watermelons. Then it came to him: *dying is a part of living*.

3

'GOD HAS HIS HAND
ON YOU, SON'

It rained so much in the weeks following Jack Cash's death that J R and the other children virtually watched the crabgrass grow as they sheltered on the front porch. When school was out, the kids and their mother hoed the fields while Ray Cash ploughed the cotton. It was gruelling work, up at 7:00am and not finishing until about 5:00pm with a short break for 'dinner' at noon. Carrie Cash remained highly emotional about Jack's death and the other children often saw her crying as she tried to hoe the cotton. She referred to 'living one day to the next' and, despite the long, hot summer, her grief continued to grow.

J R often sang in the cotton patch with his sister Reba, just as he'd done before with Jack. Johnny was able to remember the lines from the songs he'd heard on the radio and kept the other children captivated with his singing. In his early teens, J R had a high tenor voice and his family used to tease him that when he sang he could be heard for miles around. One of his favourite gospel groups was The Chuck Wagon Gang. Johnny thought the woman who sang tenor with the Gang had to be an angel and went out of his way to try and sing just like her.

J R Cash grew up virtually overnight following the death of Jack. He still had older brother Roy to occasionally sing along with. Roy had run a four-piece combo that had become popular throughout Mississippi County until he was called up to serve in World War II. They had drawn capacity crowds at local dances and, as their fame spread, they'd even been booked for programmes on KNCN, the radio station at Blytheville. Everyone was predicting a glowing future for Roy as an entertainer until he took off to fight in Europe. But Roy was the only one of his combo who came back alive. The deaths of his band members had a profound effect on Roy Cash and he never sang in public again.

There was yet more heartbreak in the Cash household when Joe, the sweetheart of J R's oldest sister Louise, was reported lost in action while serving with the Navy in the Pacific. His cruiser, the *USS Houston*, was sunk in battle in the Java Sea with 1,059 sailors on board. The Japanese had reportedly machine-gunned survivors as they struggled in the water. Louise Cash eventually recovered from her anguish and married someone else, but it was a difficult time for everyone in the family.

Ironically, Louise's lost sweetheart did actually survive his ship's sinking and ended up in a POW camp in Burma before being liberated at the end of the war. He arrived back in

Dyess expecting to pick up the pieces, only to find that Louise had married another man and moved from the area. When broken-hearted Joe bumped into J R in the centre of Dyess he begged the boy to tell him all about his sister. Johnny was delighted to be asked, because her marriage had proved a disaster and she was planning to move back to Dyess. A year later, Louise married Joe and they went on to enjoy many years of happiness together in Memphis.

J R and baby sister Reba grew much closer over the following few years. They'd often go to the movies together on Saturday afternoons and walked the quarter of a mile back and forth to the school bus together every day. Reba had the same easy-going attitude as Jack, and J R found it pleasing to bounce things off his kid sister, who was always full of good advice. She also held back from criticising his cigarette smoking, which had developed into a serious habit by the time he was twelve.

J R was developing an appetite for addictive habits. He discovered that gasoline felt *kinda* interesting if you sniffed it carefully and that became a regular pastime whenever he was in town with his friends. One day, however, he sniffed too much and it drove him to run screaming around the centre of Dyess. No one but his friends realised why Johnny had gone crazy. And the young boy didn't yet recognise his weakness for certain distractions that he could end up becoming reliant upon.

The movie theatre further fuelled young J R's interest in the country music scene – Hollywood's so-called singing cowboys Gene Autry, Tex Ritter and Roy Rogers were regularly up there on the big screen. The residents of Dyess were fed an almost nonstop diet of movies featuring those three stars. And country was starting to spread beyond its homelands too. Servicemen took the country sounds with them to far-flung corners of the globe and civilian defence workers from the South brought their love of the music into the various urban centres of war production. Country stars such as Ernest Tubb, Roy Acuff, Bob Wills and Al Dexter were soon becoming almost as popular with servicemen as Frank Sinatra and Bing Crosby.

• • • •

At school, young J R Cash didn't exactly shine at academia, although his teachers later said he daydreamed through class without too much effort, only making good grades when he really tried hard. J R certainly didn't care about homework. He hardly ever did it, preferring instead to sit and listen to the radio for hours on end. During his first semester in high school, he earned Cs and Ds, although he did pull in a few Bs in the second semester.

J R eventually graduated with one A minus. But he only worked hard at what he was interested in: English and history. In high school, he was a member of the 4H Club, the boy scouts and The Future Farmers of America. He also trained hard to become a strong swimmer, frequently powering across the strong Mississippi River on Saturday afternoons with his pals. Clearly all that training had an effect: at eighteen, he won the Arkansas State Boys Swimming Championship.

But his brother Jack always remained at the back of his

mind. His untimely death undoubtedly spurred J R on to start composing songs in his mid-teens. Many attempts were simple poetry, scribbled on to any scrap of paper that was handy. All his words were reflections of what Johnny Cash kept carefully locked away from the rest of the world.

World War II came to an end and J R and his Dyess pals continued working in the fields, his love of musical radio shows growing stronger by the day. He started to hold his own 'shows' out in the countryside for anyone who happened to be working alongside him. J R sang as they worked; the others later said it took a lot of the pain and toil out of their labour. The boys took their dinner break at noon, quickly ate and then listened from 12:30 to 1:00 to shows such as *The High Noon Roundup* over WMPS in Memphis, featuring Memphis DJ Smilin' Eddie Hill and Ira and Charlie Louvin. It was a variety show of songs, talk and lots of country comedy, which was just what the boys needed to get them over the exhaustion of their relentless work in the fields.

Despite his shyness, J R ran with the main pack of teenagers in Dyess, including J E Huff, A J Henson and Paul East. Sometimes the boys went off frogging after dark. Once, four of them hitchhiked over to Marktree to see a movie and met some girls. They stayed so late they ended the evening by walking twenty miles home in the rain.

Johnny's mom Carrie had recognised her son's talent from a young age. The daughter of a singing teacher, Carrie was determined her son should have proper voice lessons. So, for fifty cents a half-hour lesson, she engaged Miss La Vanda Mae Fielder of Lepanto, who visited the Dyess school to teach most afternoons. Mrs Cash didn't have the half dollar to spare, so she agreed to take in washing and ironing for the high-school principal and three women teachers by way of recompense.

When Johnny first appeared for a lesson, Miss Fielder asked him to sing something. He obliged her with Hank Williams's 'Lovesick Blues', then a popular country hit. Fascinated, Miss Fielder asked him to sing it over, then told him not to change his style. As it turned out, the lessons lasted only a month, because Miss Fielder admitted there wasn't much she could add to the young man's unique baritone. Soon afterwards, Johnny got himself a new portable radio, which he listened to as he worked part-time with his father clearing brush alongside the Tyronza River.

In the spring of 1947, Smilin' Eddie Hill announced over the radio that the entire cast of *The High Noon Roundup* would be making a personal appearance at Dyess High School. J R was over the moon. When the big day came, he arrived two hours early for the show and simply gazed at the group as they arrived and unloaded their equipment. When singer Charlie Louvin emerged from his dressing room and asked the loitering J R where the restroom was, it nearly turned the teenager's legs to jelly. He noticed that Charlie was munching on some soda crackers, so J R asked him if they were good for his throat.

'Nope, but they're good for your belly if you're hungry,' replied Charlie, before he disappeared into the auditorium. For years afterwards, Johnny ate soda crackers whenever he could lay his hands on them.

Before the show started, Eddie Hill walked out and asked some of the audience, including J R, if they had a request. 'Yeah, I sure do,' came the youngster's reply. 'Could you dedicate a song to my mother on the *Lonesome Valley Trio Show*?'

That day's show turned out to be beyond J R's wildest dreams. He adored the idea of hitting the road 'just like them fellas', travelling from town to town, singing for his supper. Right there and then he told one pal, 'I'll be up there some day. That's what I'm gonna be.'

After the show itself, J R waved at *The High Noon Roundup* team as they pulled off in a cloud of dust down Road 1 towards the Memphis highway. Charlie Louvin waved back, and that meant more to the young J R than anything. Then again, Charlie couldn't really help but notice J R, as he was the only one left at the auditorium, standing under a single spotlight.

Johnny Cash later recalled that day as being one of the happiest moments of his entire childhood, even though he ended up having to walk two and a half miles home in his bare feet, in the pitch dark. As he walked he sang all the songs he had heard from the stage. That evening, Carrie heard Eddie Hill and the Louvin Brothers singing 'I'll Have a New Life', 'for J R's mother'. The youngster never forgot that moment of elation and pride.

Around this time, J R began singing officially at school. Teachers regularly asked him to perform at assemblies, although he got pretty fed up over the choice of songs. After a few sessions, Johnny asked to be allowed to choose the music. 'Let me do a gospel song,' he pleaded with his teacher one day. But they wouldn't allow it and insisted on ditties such as the 'Whiffenspoof Song'. J R suggested he read one of his own poems but, after hearing the intense verse, his teacher told him, 'It's too short. Do the "Whiffenspoof Song".'

J R never had any musical accompaniment or microphone. He didn't need a mike because no one had any trouble hearing his strong, high voice. Then it was back to the rest of his school day – daydreaming, writing verses on paper and drawing pictures of tall buildings in cities he'd never seen. J R wasn't keen on sports. He missed out on the football and basketball teams because there was always work to do in the fields after school. Anyway, as a definite loner, team activities didn't really appeal to him. He preferred to be left to his dreams and aspirations.

The work in the fields never stopped. In the spring they ploughed and hoed. In the autumn and the winter, they picked the cotton. It was a relentless, simple existence, the only way of life in Dyess.

● ● ● ●

When losing one's virginity, said Queen Victoria, one must close one's eyes and think of England. Attaching a little more lyricism to the act, the great romantics, from Cervantes to Byron, saw virgins as roses and their deflowering a poem to passions that would saddle lions.

Johnny Cash's first taste of romance, his first real stirring of emotion for girls, came when he encountered school beauty Virginia North. Young J R had been daydreaming for months about how he'd take Virginia out and wine and dine her – if he'd had a car. But she was dating a boy from

Osceola, Arkansas, the county seat. Going with a boy from there was a big deal as far as the good folk of Dyess were concerned. J R watched Virginia and her sweetheart driving through Dyess one Saturday afternoon and it really infuriated him to see her with another boy. Then again, thus far he hadn't even summoned up the courage to ask her out for a date, so he only had himself to blame.

Virginia smiled at J R in school and talked a lot with him there, which had fuelled his infatuation. He wrote love letters he was never brave enough to give her. After a year of lusting after Virginia, J R was no nearer actually dating her. Some days he thought his life barely worth living if he couldn't go out with his dream girl.

Then, in the middle of all this teenage angst – the winter of 1947 – the Cash family got their first car, a 1935 Ford with mechanical brakes. Most times the brakes did not work at all and, when they did work, they worked too well. But the car was a godsend for the family – especially for Carrie and Ray, because it meant they didn't have to beg a ride into town or to church with their neighbours the Foxes, which normally meant a bumpy trip on the flatbed of a pick-up truck.

There was no heater in the old Ford. And it wasn't long before all the windows were smashed or shaken out of the car by the bumps and dips on the rough gravel roads of Dyess. As a result, whenever it was raining or very cold, the kids helped their father install slats of cardboard where the windows had once been. But it still beat Ted Fox's pick-up any day.

One rainy Saturday afternoon, when J R was about sixteen years old, he drove the car to the Dyess Cafe, the weekend gathering place for many of the town's teenagers.

Hot dogs and hamburgers were the only things most of the youngsters could afford there, plus maybe a nickel or two in the jukebox to hear Eddie Arnold or Red Foley.

J R screeched the car around the town circle, throwing up all kinds of gravel, and there, standing on the porch of the café, was Virginia North. J R slammed on the brakes – but there were no brakes. He spun the steering wheel around and slid into the porch of the café sideways. Virginia jumped to avoid getting hit and all the cardboard windows popped out on impact and dropped to the ground. Virginia couldn't keep a straight face at this chaotic arrival. Poor J R took her smile as some kind of invitation.

'How about a date tonight?' he grunted in his most macho voice, as he stepped on to the porch, soaking from the rain.

Virginia's smile faded quickly. She took a step backwards, examined the car, then looked back at J R and said, 'I might go with you some time, if you had windows in your car.' Then she twirled around and went back inside the café, leaving a bemused J R standing alone on the porch. After a few seconds, he started shaking. Who the hell did she think she was? She could go to hell. He jumped in his daddy's car, started the engine and splattered mud and gravel all over the front of the café as he fishtailed off for home. After a while, he started to feel very sorry for himself. The love of his life had not responded in the way he had hoped she might.

Finally, as he turned the car down the track towards the Cash farm, he started laughing. 'So long, Virginia North,' shouted Johnny, as he bounced along that track. 'I'll have a car with windows in it some day – and you'll be stuck pickin' cotton somewhere around Osceola!'

J R started singing a tune he'd heard on the jukebox at the café that afternoon. And it was only then that he realised for the first time that singing was a true release from the pressures of life. When he sang, he didn't have a care in the world. He needed that release. And he was going to do it even more often from now on.

● ● ● ●

Within a year, Carrie Cash had become so excited about her son's singing voice that she encouraged him to start performing all over the county. J R reminded Carrie of her father, John L Rivers, who'd led the singing at the Crossroads Methodist Church, near Kingsland, Arkansas, for forty years. J R's mother even managed to persuade their church in Dyess to allow her son to sing several 'specials'. They were soon all entranced by the teenager.

J R's voice remained high and he didn't like the key that some of the songs in church were arranged in. Even as a teenager, he already wanted his performances to be perfect. In the end, his mother had to pull him to one side in the church and gently remind him to perform whatever songs they wanted him to sing.

Carrie and many others were baffled by J R's high tenor voice. Her own father had had a resonant, bassy voice. But J R insisted he'd eventually change, although he secretly feared that he would not be able to sing once his voice had deepened.

One summer's day, after swinging an axe from dusk to dawn, J R was returning home, singing softly to himself, when he suddenly found himself face to face with his mother in the yard.

'Who's that singing in that low, booming voice?' she asked.

'That was me!' replied Johnny, almost as surprised as his momma.

That's when Carrie told him, 'God has His hand on you, son. I don't know exactly what He has in mind, but God has His hand on you.'

That evening, Johnny and the rest of his family sat down for supper at a table covered by plates of hot food. Nothing else was said about his voice. But Johnny already knew his mother was right.

4

VIVIAN AND GERMANY

J R's undoubted talent as a singer in the community gave him a bigger role within the Cash family, who continued to encourage him to develop his singing still further. He sang around the house, in the fields and even to his little sister Reba, who adored his strong, masculine voice. At high school, J R won top prize of five dollars in a singing competition with his own unique version of 'Lucky Old Sun'. The teenager was delighted and thrilled to be paid to sing in public for the first time.

But then disaster struck at school – another student accidentally stuck a pencil so deeply inside J R's inner ear for a prank that it burst part of his ear drum. This made J R's hearing abnormally acute and the youngster feared that his ability to sing would be seriously affected by it. But the accident ended up having the opposite effect: J R discovered that his abnormal hearing simply intensified his inherent feeling for verse and song.

With the after-effects of World War II still rippling throughout the world, a lot of J R's classmates enlisted in the services. At first, he decided that wasn't the life for him and tried to find work locally so he could stay close to his beloved family. But work in rural areas such as Dyess was hard to come by. J R spent many months hitchhiking to neighbouring counties in search of a job. He didn't care what sort of work he took, just so long as it helped bring in a wage to help towards the upkeep of the family. Father Ray told his son it was more important for J R to get himself a proper career than worry about the family, but J R wanted to make his contribution.

It turned out to be a very difficult period in his life, sometimes involving travelling upwards of a hundred miles on the off chance of a job in a factory or a mill, not even knowing for sure if work was available. Often he'd find that all the positions had already been grabbed by people who lived nearby.

J R eventually got so desperate he travelled with a group of Dyess youths migrating north to earn a steady wage in the automobile factories. Frank McKinney, who'd been a barber in Dyess, persuaded J R to go along. They hitched a ride with mailman Dewey Cox to the railroad town of Wilson, where they took a train to Memphis before hopping on a Greyhound bus to the automobile centre of the nation, Detroit. J R and the others from Dyess found rooms in a boarding house in the city and then he took himself straight off to apply for a job at the Fisher Body Plant, in Pontiac.

Johnny later explained: 'When I applied for the job, the man told me: "You're not going to be like the other young guys from the South who come up and think they're gonna get rich in advance, are you? Most of them work a couple of weeks or maybe a month, and then go home to Mama."' J R insisted he was serious and landed a job on a punch press, working the day shift. That meant getting up at 4:30am for breakfast – a slice of toast – and then walking a mile and a half to the plant every day.

Johnny recalled: 'I couldn't stand the work. It was such drudgery, lifting those hoods hour after hour, man, I didn't do anything after work but get to bed. I had been 150 pounds, at six feet. I lost ten pounds in two weeks – I was so skinny. It was such a change of pace from living on the farm. Evening you worked on a farm, but at least you got good food.'

Detroit seemed like a foreign country to young J R. He'd never stayed the night more than fifty miles from home in his entire life – and he was virtually broke. 'Then the one day I had off in two weeks, I caught a bad cold. The woman who ran the boarding house put me in bed and gave me a glass of wine. It was the first liquor I ever tasted. I nearly got sick on it. It was so horrible I never did finish it,' recalled Johnny.

Back at work the following day, J R was still feeling very sick. A few days later he cut his right forearm on a bonnet. That proved to be the final straw. J R went straight to the medical dispensary, where he had the wound treated, and decided to quit the job later that same day. He hitchhiked home with another guy from Dyess, with $150 in wages on him. It was more money than he'd ever had in his entire life.

But in Dyess, J R was back to square one again. He took

a job at the same factory in the nearby town of Evadale where his father now worked. His job involved cleaning up the vats and sweeping the floors. But he hated it so much he quit after just two weeks. His mother and father wondered how on earth their son was going to survive if he couldn't hold a job down.

• • • •

In July, 1950, J R, now eighteen, proved everyone wrong by going to Memphis and enlisting in the Air Force; on the application form he claimed his civilian occupation had been 'buttermaker'. Dad Ray Cash was delighted. He'd been a World War I vet and the Cash family men had served in the armed forces for the previous five generations.

On July 7, 1950, J R Cash reported for duty with the USAF. He was immediately told he'd have to use a full first name and so was officially referred to as John. He started his Air Force training in Texas. With the Korean War barely three weeks old, training facilities were so poor that the usual thirteen weeks of training were cut to seven. The newly named John Cash was in the 3712 Training Squadron and was warned he could end up in Korea. 'I can remember the fears I had about going into combat. I didn't want to kill. I guess I was really a conscientious objector. But I wouldn't have refused to go if I'd been called to.' John used his interest in radio to enrol in radio operating school. He turned out to have a good grasp for communications.

On September 21, 1950, John Cash began six months of specialist communications training at Mississippi's Kessler

Air Force Base. He picked up Morse code so quickly that he finished the course four weeks ahead of the other students. His instructors were impressed and they selected him for the USAF Security Service, who monitored international flight radio traffic. In 1951, the Security Service had squadrons deployed in Germany, Japan and the Brooks AFB, Texas, where John had just been trained.

John's impressive skills as a radio intercept operator helped give him a lot more confidence on the social front. The gangly kid from Arkansas was genuinely proud of what he was doing. He liked the comradeship of his fellow airmen. It was the first time he'd made friends with anyone outside his own community and some of them even had similar musical interests to his own.

John had seen a lot of new things, new places and new people but he still remained a country boy at heart. A lot of his barrack-room pals were desperate to go to Korea and see some action, but John wasn't especially anxious to start killing people. That said, any place represented a new adventure, and from that point of view he looked forward to active service eagerly.

In barracks, John took a lot of ribbing from northern boys about his accent and Arkansas expressions. He took it all in good spirit and gave as good as he got. Some of his fellow Southerners got into fights with loud-mouthed Brooklyn types, but John was too big to tangle with. He also minded his own business and kept out of other people's way – except when he had money and then he'd play cards and shoot crap with the hardest of them. John wasn't a flashy gambler, but he was cool and steady, and won more often than he lost.

John's tour of duty in the San Antonio area of Texas lasted until rumours began flying around that his group were shipping out to Korea within five days. Then they heard they'd be going to Hawaii first for more training. Next, they were informed that it'd be Japan to check out new equipment. Their potential destinations changed with monotonous regularity.

One night, John and some buddies drove into town from their base at the Jefferson Barracks, in San Antonio, for some fun. They ended up in a local hotspot called the St Mary's Rollerskating Rink. The boys caused chaos slipping and sliding all over the ring, and John bumped into a pretty seventeen-year-old brunette called Vivian Liberto. He immediately asked Vivian for a date, even though he'd just been told he'd be leaving for Germany imminently.

Vivian's father Thomas was in the insurance business in San Antonio and was also an amateur magician; the Italian Liberto family had a built-in musical heritage which was a vitally important part of their lives. That's why John and Vivian hit it off right from the moment they met. The Libertos immediately took to John and he felt completely at home with their warm family, even though he knew nothing about their favourite music, opera. During the days before he departed, John managed to see Vivian every day. They went dancing, took in some movies and went rollerskating again and John also enjoyed Mrs Liberto's superb cooking.

Less than a month later, John left a heartbroken Vivian to be shipped off to Germany to serve with the Social Service division of the Air Force. He promised his sweetheart he'd stay in touch, and believed that if he could keep the romance going on a long-distance level then they might eventually marry. The two came to an 'understanding', which translated roughly meant that she was his girl and he was her guy.

Just before leaving for Germany, John visited his family in Dyess. It was an emotional final trip home and on the day of his departure from Arkansas, he borrowed his father's 1946 Pontiac to drive with his mom and eleven-year-old brother Tommy to catch a train from Memphis.

En route, they stopped at an automobile sales company where older brother Roy worked as a mechanic. John parked the car in front of the garage and they all chatted with Roy until John started worrying he might miss his train. When they walked outside, the car was gone and it was only then John remembered he'd left the key in the ignition. He phoned the police, but there was no time to look for the car because he had to catch that train.

Johnny later recalled: 'Oh, man, when I got on that train, I felt like the world had come to an end. It was a terrible feeling to leave Mama there on the street and our car stolen.' The car eventually turned up a month later with a lot of miles on the clock.

Airman Cash's fortunes improved after he arrived at his new home of Landsberg, Germany. With Europe split in two between the so-called superpowers and their respective allies, John had the task of helping the West keep close tabs on the communists. He never fully explained his role, as it was classified top secret by the military and he always rigidly and patriotically avoided providing details. But military experts insist that radio intercept officers such as John Cash helped save hundreds if not thousands of lives during the ten years following the end of World War II. There were even occasions when their quick thinking and expertise probably helped prevent a World War III, as tensions between the West and the communist eastern bloc countries worsened so much during that period.

John found Germany a refreshing experience. He'd never been abroad before and was intrigued by the German people. Initially, he gravitated towards the non-drinking servicemen at the base, as opposed to the wild ones who usually spent their three-day passes going out on alcoholic binges. Some of his closest pals played guitar, banjo and harmonica and were raised on hillbilly and gospel music, just as John had been. Others were more than happy to talk religion for hours on end.

Johnny later explained, 'We were pretty rough and raw musically. Invariably, whenever we had a session, we'd always come back to gospel music. We'd sing a three- and four-part harmony before the night was over, and those songs had a way of taking us back home.'

It was in Germany that John bought his first guitar and taught himself to 'pick'. He began to formulate his unique playing style, which was to become so famous in later years. His Air Force friend Orville Rigdon, from Louisiana, helped teach him how to play.

In Germany, John began visiting war memorials for the first time and always alone. He went a total of fifteen times to one site where Nazi machine gunners had slaughtered five hundred Jews. Sometimes, John would just sit on his own and cry his eyes out. He couldn't really understand why he felt so moved by the place. He'd never even known anyone who was a Jew; he simply felt so bad about what had happened. Johnny Cash later speculated as to whether it was his rumoured Indian blood that had made him feel so emotional about that war memorial. People who lived in or near Indian reservations would understand what he meant. 'The Jew, the Indian and the Negro,' said Johnny many years later, 'allowed their images to be built up. That just shows me they are even better people. Some people might think that makes it look like they're weaker people but, to me, it's that they're better people.'

It was in Germany that John first started drinking alcohol. After proudly purchasing another guitar he stopped at a tavern in a snowstorm on the way back to his base and fortified himself with a few steins of German beer. He later recalled: 'Then I walked back four miles to the base, me and my beer and my guitar in the snow. I'd drunk enough beer to keep me from freezing. It was a blizzard and I kept losing my way. They said I looked like a snowman when I walked through the gate. My hair was covered in snow. I don't know why I didn't freeze to death.'

John also grew increasingly fascinated by the electric nightlife in Germany that seemed to exist in every major town. The inexperienced John was intrigued by the gaudy bars and the buxom women hanging out in most of them. His Air Force buddies would regularly rib him about his lack of experience with alcohol and women. He was nearly twenty years of age and his brief fling with Vivian was the only relationship he'd ever had – and that had been kept on a very respectable level.

Beer rapidly became the soothing liquid of choice for

John, and the church and his hometown of Dyess began to feel a million miles away. Drinking opened up a completely new social scene for John; he and his pals hung out at bars where women and beer were served on tap. For the first time in his life he began using profanities. And many more ominous habits soon followed. As the nights wore on, Cognac would replace beer. Chapel visits back at the base became a rarity. John was slipping, as he put it, 'from the arms of the Lord into the hands of the demon deception'.

The nonstop boozing often turned drunken fishing trips with Air Force pals into deep, philosophical discussions about religion. A favourite spot was the village of Oberammergau, a breathtakingly beautiful place surrounded by snow-capped mountains. John considered that hard liquor was acting as a stimulant as far as his feelings about religion were concerned. Sometimes he'd command centre stage and try – through beer and Cognac – to convince his buddies they were all sinning, only to be shouted down amid a sea of boos and hisses.

Around that time, John found himself facing regular sleepless nights – he couldn't tell if they were brought about by the alcohol or by his deeply disturbed conscience. Often, he'd get out of bed and sit at his desk and vent his confusion through his poetry. He kept his work secret at first, afraid that his compatriots might label him a little odd for writing such intense pieces. But then one highly sensitive friend persuaded John to send some of his verses to the servicemen's magazine *Stars and Stripes*, where they were accepted and printed a number of times.

John's invaluable Air Force job was proving exhausting

and highly stressful. Most of the time he sat in front of a sophisticated receiver, locating and listening through earphones to the coded ground and air traffic movements of the Soviet Air Force. It took a genuinely steady hand and keen hearing to calibrate the frequency used by the Soviets.

Details of Johnny Cash's top-secret work have never before been disclosed but, with the collapse of eastern bloc communist nations in the late '80s, that important role can be revealed for the first time. He was secretly sent around Europe at short notice on special missions to spy on the enemy. As someone who could filter through static and copy down over forty words a minute, Airman Cash was in big demand.

In June, 1953, he was one of a thirteen-man unit sent to Italy for three months. The team's main task was to set up complex electrical scanning equipment in a bean field near the Italian town of Foggia. It was around the time of the Rosenberg spy executions back in the US and the town had staged a huge anti-American protest march. John and his comrades were staying undercover as ordinary Air Force personnel in a local hotel. They were so scared by death threats made to them in letters left at the hotel that they each went out and bought a pistol for self-defence. One overambitious second lieutenant ordered John not to walk around Foggia with a weapon and tried to take the gun away from him. Fierce words were exchanged, during which John threatened to whip his superior officer with the weapon if he didn't 'butt out'. Eventually the officer gave up – he didn't even report John or his colleagues because he feared they'd beat him up if he did.

Foggia's hatred of Americans was fuelled by the fact that

John and his fellow airmen were monitoring Russian and eastern European troop and air movements late at night in the field where their equipment was set up. This meant late-night movements through the streets of Foggia, sparking further suspicion amongst the locals. The USAF operation in Foggia was eventually deemed an overwhelming success and John was duly promoted to chief of his forty-man shift back at Landsberg. The work was becoming ever more gruelling, however: his superiors were reluctant to relieve him on complex assignments because of his widely recognised superior skills. Sometimes he worked straight 24-hour shifts.

John was considered by his buddies to be a loner who rarely shared his frustrations and innermost thoughts with others. Some nights that accumulation of inner tension exploded into dark, disturbing incidents. One time, the frustration grew so bad that he picked up his typewriter, threw it out of the window of his second-floor office and started crying. John was eventually sent to the medical dispensary, given a couple of aspirins and told to take the rest of the night off. If the same thing had happened today, John would have been given patient and understanding counselling, and booked in to see the base psychiatrist.

John regularly wrote home about his adventures in Europe and enclosed relevant snapshots with explanations scrawled across the back of them. Since arriving in Germany, he'd also corresponded almost daily with Vivian Liberto back in San Antonio, Texas. He was lonely enough in Germany to regularly phone her long distance and eventually he suggested they should get married. Her father wouldn't agree to let Vivian go off to Germany for a wedding, but she agreed to marry when John returned to the US. Vivian's parents were extremely protective of their teenage daughter, who was by now working for an insurance company in San Antonio. A typical day for her consisted of catching the bus at 6:30am, when it was still dark, to get to church before going to work. Her mother would stand out on the porch and watch her until she safely caught the bus outside their home.

Back in Germany, John's boozing began to seriously alarm his small group of buddies. And with all that alcohol came another much more worrying side-effect – his now legendary temper began to scratch the surface.

Life as a serviceman in Germany wasn't really about fighting or engaging an imaginary enemy, and there were potentially lucrative sidelines for those who wanted to take advantage of them. For example, John had got himself caught up in a mini-black-market syndicate that bought cigarettes at US prices inside the base and then sold them for five times that price in the surrounding towns. Air Force officials ignored such activities just so long as they did not get out of control. And to the lower ranks such as John and his pals, the extra income was vitally important. On one occasion, John strolled past the security gates at the exit to the base and was stopped by two wise-assed MPs; it took all his self-control not to shout back at them when they pulled him up. One of the guards insisted John couldn't take his cartons of cigarettes with him. At that point the young serviceman felt a rush of anger, something that in later life would cause him all sorts of problems. John later explained: 'They took the cigarettes for themselves. I invited them both out at once, and I knocked them down a fifty-foot embankment. I knocked one's teeth out and I broke the other's nose. They ran off. It was the only fight I ever really had. Oh, I had some brawls, but I never did get hurt.'

Quietly spoken loner John was the last person any of his pals expected to get involved in a brawl. John refused to fully elaborate to his friends on what exactly had happened. A pattern was emerging in which he would accumulate the tension and pressure within himself and then suddenly explode. It became his trademark in later, more difficult years.

John knew what he was doing and where he wanted to be, but this fury was a part of him that he couldn't understand or even always control. Often he found himself retreating more and more into himself and that prevented him from trusting any person outside his beloved family.

A number of violent incidents soon followed, including a fight with a paratrooper in a German honkytonk bar during which a German girl stuck a pen in John's eardrum. His hearing was already impaired from that earlier incident with the pencil when he was still at school. Fortunately, this latest injury didn't harm his hearing or his abilities as a singer.

Most fights in Germany were over women. German girls were desperate to please their American visitors and John found it difficult to handle their sexual openness. He also still had Vivian on his mind, which made him feel guilty, and that in turn sparked his temper to erupt. If he did cheat on Vivian, he kept it very much to himself. Another time John almost got caught up in a very nasty scene outside a nightclub when four airmen tried to drag a girl down an alleyway after she kept making eyes at them all on the dance floor. The men wanted John to join them, but he refused and left the scene before anything actually happened.

After four years in the Air Force, John Cash – despite being promoted to staff sergeant – did not re-enlist and was honourably discharged on July 3, 1954. He rushed back to the transient barracks where he'd been quartered, grabbed his bag and his guitar and ran out to start the long journey home.

The people John loved most of all in the world formed a special welcoming committee at Memphis Airport. Even the gorgeous Vivian Liberto was there, her huge brown eyes moist with tears of joy as she embraced the big, handsome guy who'd bowled her over in a San Antonio rollerskating rink three years earlier.

Tears also trickled down Carrie's cheeks as she threw her arms around the broad shoulders of her son. Then her eyes narrowed. 'You're too thin,' said Carrie. 'You need some good home cookin'.' John laughed happily and kissed her again.

Ray Cash shook his son's hand warmly and clapped him on the shoulder. 'You look great,' he said. 'It's been a long time.' Truth be told, the booze and complications of life in a foreign land had actually made John an even more troubled person than the one his family remembered. They noticed he was constantly fidgeting and spent hours every day just sitting in silence on the porch outside the Cash home in Dyess. Any attempt by his mother or father to try and find out about his problems met with little response.

Ray Cash knew instinctively that something had happened to John. He noticed John's now crooked nose (caused by a fight in Germany) and on his face was a large scar, which he claimed had been caused by a drunken German doctor removing a cyst.

John Cash spent many days in reunions with family, relatives and friends. There was a lot of singing, and Cash had the chance to display his new talents as a guitar player. Sweetheart Vivian went everywhere with him, and he proudly showed her off as the girl he was going to marry. Everyone complimented him on having such a beautiful girlfriend.

Then he headed down to San Antonio, Texas, and Vivian's family. Her father Joe approved of the marriage plans, but told the couple they should wait a month. 'He wanted them both to be absolutely sure it was the right decision,' one family member later explained.

John was happy to wait. It seemed a small sacrifice to make for the first uplifting event in his life since the death of his brother, Jack. John Cash genuinely wanted to provide the sort of happy family life his parents had so successfully achieved, although he wasn't certain he had the same strength of character as his father. Only time would tell …

5

BAD SALESMAN. GOOD SINGER

On Saturday, August 7, 1954, John Cash married his sweetheart Vivian in a small ceremony at St Ann's Church, in San Antonio, Texas. Though he was now a civilian, John's only 'suit' was his woollen Air Force blues. With temperatures soaring into the nineties, John came close to fainting. Vivian's uncle – a priest called Father Vincent Liberto – officiated the marriage ceremony with John's older brother Roy acting as best man.

Then came the reception on the terrace of the nearby St Anthony's Hotel. There are no weddings in the world like Italian weddings, and the festivities surrounding the marriage of Vivian Liberto to John Cash certainly lived up to that reputation, with dancing, wine and endless songs. It seemed to John that everyone there was a singer with a better than average voice. He heard operatic arias in solo, duets, quartets, sextets and massed choruses. He even heard rollicking Italian folk songs and won the hearts of everyone when, after one of these renditions, he exclaimed spontaneously: 'Why, that's hillbilly music – with an Italian accent!'

At his new father-in-law's urging, John played his guitar and sang – to his own accompaniment – several traditional country tunes. Everyone loved his performance. One of the male guests then borrowed John's guitar and played a fiery tune that sparked a wild rush to the dance floor. John never forgot the sound that guest plucked out of his five-dollar guitar and he'd use the same playing methods himself in later years.

Afterwards, the happy couple climbed in his brother Roy's car and headed off to Memphis to start their new lives together. It was all a dream come true for John Cash. Despite all the boozing and high jinks in Germany he'd continued living in hope that Vivian would eventually marry him. Her devout Catholicism had been a problem at first. John's parents Ray and Carrie had seriously worried that the differences between their religions were far too wide. But John and Vivian had assured their respective parents: 'We worship the same God. There is only one Jesus.' John later admitted he knew religion might be a problem for the two of them, although he was convinced he'd overcome it.

John agreed that all their children should be brought up as Catholics and promised to attend Catholic church with them. That meant a crash course in his new religion. His parents were surprised, but so delighted by their son's new-found happiness that they didn't interfere. Within days of the marriage, John started a six-month instruction course in Catholicism with a priest in Memphis. However, throughout

John still kept up his commitment to the religion of his birth and every Sunday he'd attend 9:00am mass with Vivian before rushing over to the Protestant services at 10:30am.

Perhaps surprisingly, John managed to shake off his reliance on alcohol within a short time of arriving back from Germany. He announced to friends and family that he never really liked drinking in the first place and found it easy to abstain once again. He was clearly determined to make his marriage a long-lasting success.

Not having a job left John Cash with an emptiness in his life following his discharge from the Air Force, where he'd always been so busy. For four years, he'd not had to worry about supporting anyone but now it felt as if he was back to square one. John eventually got a job as an appliance salesman at a local store called Home Equipment, in Memphis. In the evenings, he'd also hit the streets and go door to door through rich and poor suburban neighbourhoods in a desperate bid to earn extra commission. It was a gruelling job – John had wrongly presumed selling would be easy, while, in fact, it couldn't have been harder.

While working the shacks in Orange Mound, a squalid black ghetto area of Memphis, he met Gus Cannon, an old black handyman who sang his own songs to the accompaniment of a five-string banjo. John subsequently laid out his route every week so he'd end up at Gus Cannon's place. 'I couldn't sell anything anyway, so I thought I might as well sit and listen to Gus,' Johnny later recalled. Ironically, one of the handyman's songs, 'Walk Right In', later became a commercial hit in 1962, though Gus Cannon himself made only a pittance from it.

Not even Gus's musical talents could kill the sheer drudgery of John's salesman job. One day, after having a front door slammed in his face at least a hundred times, he knocked on one last house. A lady answered.

'Don't s'ppose you want to buy anythin' either, do you, Ma'am?' muttered an exhausted John.

'Depends what you're selling.'

'Nothin' special,' came John's reply.

'Then why d'you knock on my door, young man?' she asked.

'So you'd make my day complete by tellin' me no.'

'You get away from my door or I'll call the police,' the woman spluttered.

'How 'bout a used washing machine? Only had nine previous owners,' replied John, laughing out loud as the woman slammed the door in his face.

As Johnny later explained: 'I really thought I'd be successful at sellin'. I had every intention of being so. But I hated tryin' to convince people that they should have somethin' that they really didn't want. I felt dishonest. I hated every minute of goin' door to door. I'd go down to the poorest sections of town, but I might as well have told them, "Oh, you don't want to buy anythin' anyway."' John Cash couldn't help his streak of basic decency. It had been ingrained in him from childhood. It was a blessing and a curse but ultimately it drove him onwards in life.

John and his young bride Vivian lived in a tiny apartment on a street called East Morland, in the centre of Memphis. It consisted of just three rooms and a bath and cost $55 (£30) a month. They rarely went out, except to the local movie theatre. But they had each other and that was the driving force behind John's determination to survive. Just to get to the kitchen of the apartment you had to walk up a third flight of stairs in addition to the two-storey climb in the first place. When Vivian became pregnant a few months after their wedding, John immediately moved them to a ground-floor apartment, which wouldn't be so exhausting for the mother-to-be.

But inside himself John Cash was tearing himself apart with frustration because he still harboured dreams of one day becoming a musical success. He could not keep his mind on anything else. The only aspect of his salesman job he enjoyed was sitting in his green '54 Plymouth listening to the radio. At night, he'd lie awake listening to those music shows outside the front doors he couldn't be bothered to knock on. Back home he started belting out a few of his own songs for his friends and family.

As John's frustration mounted, he tried to talk his way into a job as a disc jockey on WMCA, a radio station based in Corinth, Mississippi. That ended with some friendly words from a station head who advised John to enrol in a place called Keegan's School of Broadcasting in Memphis. 'Come and see me when you've finished the course,' he added. John took his advice and enrolled at Keegan's School, training to be a staff announcer, news broadcaster and disc jockey, although he only attended part-time because he had to carry on working to provide for his pregnant wife.

John adored his time at Keegan's – especially the hours when he was allowed to play the part of disc jockey. Then his brother Roy introduced him to two mechanic friends called

Marshall Grant and Luther Perkins, who played guitars in their spare time. Every night between five-thirty and six when business was slack, Grant and Perkins would retire to the back of the car shop to play a few tunes together. The three would-be musicians soon became firm friends and began practising together at each other's homes, much to Vivian's obvious irritation.

Marshall Grant was soon convinced his partnership with John and Luther could lead to big things. He later described it in almost holy terms: 'That first day I looked up and saw Roy Cash and his brother Johnny walkin' in here, it flashed across me. You'd describe it as if you seen God. It sent little chill bumps all over me. Johnny was walkin' toward me and I felt some way, somehow, that there was something we had in common, you know? And then we went over to talk to Luther Perkins and we instantly became like blood brothers right on the spot before he even left the building that first day.'

Soon friends and neighbours started popping round to hear the three new pals performing. John made a point of singing all the most popular country songs of the time, but was also careful to choose the ones that suited his voice best. Marshall joined in singing tenor on the gospel songs. He was from the mountains of North Carolina and had picked up many tunes from the radio just like John. Marshall had eleven brothers and sisters and was at one time the North Carolina state champion cotton picker. He didn't drink (not even coffee) or smoke and his only known vice was to chew the occasional piece of gum on stage. His only weakness was dynamite – but more about that later.

Then there was Luther Perkins, with his unique guitar

technique of deadening one string and letting the others ring, creating the impression of a rhythm and lead guitar playing at the same time. The son of a Baptist preacher from Mississippi, Luther had just as strong a presence as the other two but he didn't tell anyone much about himself. None of them ever forgot the first night all three played together at Luther's house on Nathan Street, Memphis. John played guitar and sang Hank Snow's classic 'Moving On'. All three wives sat and talked and drank coffee on the porch as if it was a perfectly normal evening. None of them realised the significance of what they were about to achieve.

John was so broke at this time that he rarely had enough money to pay the monthly rent in one chunk. His job as a salesman was on a commission-only basis and he wasn't selling anything. Often brother Roy or pals Luther or Marshall loaned John $50 to take the homesick Vivian on one of her frequent journeys back to her home town, San Antonio, Texas.

Not surprisingly, John's failure as a salesman only intensified his natural restlessness. He was frustrated and confused about what he could and could not do well. Music was fast becoming his only release from the drudgery of life. Every time he got together with the boys it was an escape from all his problems. Music was John's way out. His escape route.

One night, John suggested he and his two pals try playing different instruments instead of just three acoustic guitars. Luther went out and borrowed an electric guitar. John, since he did most of the singing, announced he'd pump out the rhythm on his five-dollar German guitar. Marshall Grant borrowed a bass. Johnny later recalled: 'It was a big wooden upright bass. I remember, when we got it, we didn't know how to tune it. A musician friend didn't know either, but he came back with a diagram, and we all got together one evening and figured out how to tune that bass. We marked the notes on it with adhesive tape. Luther played a D on his guitar and we marked it where it was on the neck of the bass with the tape.'

Like Marshall, John and Luther were self-taught, but in country music that lack of formal training was not relevant. In any case, they more than made up for it by practising for many hours together every week.

John Cash's first public appearance with his group was at a church in North Memphis. They had been invited to do a guest spot by a neighbour who loved the sound of their music. All three decided they should dress the same for their first concert, but none of them had a decent suit and the only coloured shirts they had which were all alike were black. 'Black will be better for church, anyway,' insisted John. All three turned up in black shirts and trousers and thus the legend of the 'Man in Black' was born. For the rest of his life, Johnny always refused to elaborate further on why he constantly wore black. He simply offered the explanation: 'Black is better for church.'

A few weeks after that first low-key appearance, John and his pals put on a benefit show for a friend of Marshall's who'd been injured in a hydroplane accident in nearby Hot Springs. They performed in the back room of a drive-thru restaurant on Summer Avenue, in Memphis. This was the first time an audience had paid to hear John sing, although he got none of the money himself that night.

The overwhelmingly enthusiastic response John and his two pals, Marshall and Luther, got from those first few performances encouraged John to feel that he should pursue his musical ambitions. He knew that singing town-to-town would be as exhausting as selling door-to-door, but he also believed that it would be the making of his career. All this raw experience would help him learn how to seize and hold an audience years before he'd earned their loyalty and adoration. The next important step was to get a gig on the radio and that was no easy task for an unknown country boy.

Back in the real world, John Cash's work as a salesman was going from bad to worse. He often had to go out and sell at night, frequently in the dark and dingy ghettos of Memphis. Vivian sometimes escorted him and sat in their car with the doors locked while John approached residents for potential sales. The only reason John hung on to his job was because his boss, George Bates, liked him. Eventually, however, even Bates could see that things weren't working out. He called the failing salesman into his office and asked him outright what he really wanted to do with his life.

'I wanna sing on the radio, maybe some day make a record,' replied John with deep sincerity.

'And how you goin' to get on the radio, son?'

'Someone's gotta sponsor me. Costs a dollar a minute for a fifteen-minute show, sir.'

George Bates leaned back gently in his seat and scratched his chin.

'Well, maybe I might be prepared to help you, John.'

Cash was dumbstruck. He'd never in his wildest dreams imagined his boss would help launch his musical career. So it was that Home Equipment sponsored a radio show featuring Cash with his friends Luther Perkins and Marshall Grant on Saturday afternoons on KWEM – from 2:00pm to 2:15pm.

Around this time, John tried to take a long hard, realistic look at his life. What kind of a future could he really offer his wife? He could farm, but what use was that in a city? In any case, farming off the land wasn't enough to support a family in those hard times. What else could he do? Well, he thought to himself, he could play a mean guitar and sing country, in his opinion, as well as any country singer on the radio. That's when John Cash made his choice. There was no other road to follow: 'I decided to try 'n' make a livin' singin' and playin' shows,' he explained many years later. So he got in his Plymouth and drove all over north-eastern Arkansas, dropping into theatres and schoolhouses, asking them if he could book himself in to play a show. John even took his father Ray to one of his first live performances in the farming town of Etowa, twenty miles from the family home in Dyess.

Etowa's only entertainment centre was an old wooden building next to a crummy beer joint on the edge of town. About forty or fifty people crammed into the barn. The charge was fifty cents for adults and 25 for children. Onstage before the performance, John pulled out his comb and ran it through his hair, in a style not a million miles away from that adopted by another up-and-coming star, Elvis Presley. Then Marshall threw the comb on the floor, pulled out a blank pistol and shot at it as if it had lice. The audience lapped it up.

Back in Memphis, John's radio show only ran for a short time, but the exposure led to more live appearances across the city for the group. Then Cash decided to corner Perkins and Grant about the next step in their musical career.

'How 'bout we head over to Sun Records and see if they'll let us make a record?' asked the ever-enthusiastic John. His two partners rolled their eyes but played along with him. It was worth a shot.

Sun Records in Memphis had been grinding out what were referred to as 'race records' in the Fifties. That meant rhythm & blues music specially geared as a bridge between traditional Negro music and what would later become the soul music of the 1960s. The advent of early rock'n'roll was about to push Sun Records into a lucrative marketplace – combining gritty black blues music with the rural electrification of the white country sound. The director of the label, Sam Phillips, had recently recorded a truck driver from East Tupelo, Mississippi, the aforementioned Elvis Presley, marketing him as a white blues singer and taking advantage of his appeal to both men and women.

John Cash had his sights firmly focused on recording some songs and he was convinced Sam Phillips and his Sun Records were the perfect place for him to launch the next stage of his career.

6

SAM PHILLIPS AND SUN

John Cash showed an impressive ability to get to the people who mattered. When he finally got the legendary Sam Phillips on the phone, however, the music man was kind but also very firm. 'I love those hymns and gospel songs, too, John, but we have to sell records to stay in business. We're a small company and we can't afford to speculate on a new artist singing gospel,' Phillips explained to the enthusiastic young singer.

'I'm gonna record them, Mr Phillips. I don't know when, but I know I'm gonna do it,' replied John.

'Well, good luck to you,' Phillips said, and hung up.

But John Cash wouldn't take no for an answer. He tried to arrange a personal meeting with Phillips, but couldn't get past his secretary. Eventually, Cash got Phillips on the phone again. Phillips told John he admired his persistence and, after a lot of pleading, he agreed to give John an audition.

Cash and his two partners were literally shaking in their boots with nerves when they appeared at Sun Records, in Memphis, on the big day. To make matters worse, they had A W Kernodle, a fourth, occasional member of the group with them. He'd sometimes played his steel guitar with them and John believed this extra dimension might just sell the group to Phillips. But Kernodle was so nervous that he walked out of the studio before they'd even played a note. John ignored the setback and he and his two pals almost instantly broke into their catalogue of songs, including the gospel 'Belshazzar' and 'Hey Porter'.

Sam Phillips was impressed by what he heard and told the trio he'd sign them up if they could provide the perfect flip-side song to 'Hey Porter'. This was enough to convince John he was on the way to stardom. The moment he got home he started knocking out a new song. The final result became known as the classic 'Cry, Cry, Cry'.

Another audition date was set, but Sam Phillips didn't show up. Cash and the others were heartbroken and wondered if he'd really meant what he'd said earlier. It was only several months later that Phillips finally met up with them again. However, that delay gave John and the boys enough time to experiment and strengthen their sound. John began sticking a piece of paper between his guitar strings and the neck frets so that, when he strummed, the rattle of the paper created a noise like a snare drum. Meanwhile, Luther worked on duplicating both a lead and a rhythm guitar. He hit a note, muffled the strings with the heel of his right hand and hit again. The booming noise counterpointed Johnny Cash's songs from that moment on.

Marshall Grant splashed out $44.65 (£28) on an electric amplifier from a local department store. It took two weeks to arrive, leaving the group terrified that the next Sun Records audition might come before the amplifier. Finally, they met up with Sam Phillips one winter evening in a small studio on the corner of Marshall and Union Avenues, in Memphis. It was only the twenty-first time that Marshall Grant had even played on a track with his own upright bass. As Johnny later explained: 'The recording session was the first we'd ever seen. We'd never been in a recording studio, and we were green and scared.'

But Phillips was upbeat: 'I'll give you a contract,' he told them. 'But I'll release what I feel is right for the market.' John looked at the others and realised this was too big an opportunity to miss out on. He agreed to Phillips's conditions and the Johnny Cash recording phenomenon was under way. Sam Phillips insisted on 'Hey Porter' and 'Cry, Cry, Cry' for the group's first single.

The next day, John wandered by to see Marshall at work at the automobile repair shop. Sam Phillips had just telephoned and wanted to know what they were going to call themselves.

'How about the Tennessee Three?' volunteered John.

Marshall gave it an instant thumbs down. Since John was doing all the singing, it ought to be John Cash and the Tennessee Two he insisted, though, in fact, none of them was actually from Tennessee.

But Sam Phillips wasn't completely happy with that suggestion either. With an eye on the teenage market, he suggested that *Johnny* Cash and the Tennessee Two had a better ring to it. John was puzzled. He thought it might make him sound too young. Phillips reassured John that, at twenty-three years old, he could afford to be 'Johnny'.

When Johnny Cash signed his Sun recording contract, the complicated legal jargon amused him. 'You know where it always says in a contract "for one dollar and other considerations"? Well, I signed that contract and I stood around for an hour waiting for them to give me that dollar. They never gave it to me, and I didn't want to ask for it. Finally, I left. I had just fifteen cents in my pocket when I walked out of Sun Records. It wasn't enough for a pack of cigarettes so, when this panhandler stuck his hand out, I gave it to him. That may sound like a story, but it's the truth.' Many years later, one of Johnny's many fan magazines printed a story that Johnny had run out of petrol just as his car rolled up outside his home after signing that historic first contract. The story was repeated across the world, but Johnny has always insisted it never happened that way.

The group's first record was cut a few weeks later, but not released immediately, so Johnny Cash and the Tennessee Two continued with their daytime jobs and bided their time. They even appeared from the flatbed of a truck that drove across Memphis advertising an automobile sale at a local Ford dealership. On Saturday afternoons, the threesome cruised Memphis, balancing on a swaying 8-by-10-foot flatbed and tried to perform a few of their songs over a scratchy public address system. It wasn't a runaway success, but it did bring in fifty bucks to be split three ways.

The minute the first pressing of their 78rpm record finally came off the presses, Johnny dashed over to the Sun studio, grabbed a copy and took it straight to Bob Neal at WMPS, a local radio station. Neal liked the record the moment it started to play. As the yellow Sun record label went round and round, Johnny finally realised that his dream was coming true. Neal flipped the record and played the other side. Then he went back to the 'A' side. He was hooked and Johnny Cash had climbed up the first rung in the showbusiness ladder.

A few days later, group member Marshall was driving to work one morning in his 1940 green Plymouth and listening to WHHM when he heard the disc jockey say: 'I gotta new record here on the Sun label and it's a gas.' Next Marshall heard 'Cry, Cry, Cry' blaring out. He couldn't believe his ears. Then the disc jockey came on air again: 'I dunno these boys but I never heard anythin' come in with such a different sound. It won't be the last time you hear o' them.'

That first single sold a hundred thousand copies across the South. In June that year, Johnny got his first royalty checque from Sun – for $2.41. And out of that he had to pay $15 dues to the American Federation of Musicians! Brother Roy's wife Wandene felt so sorry for Johnny she offered to lend him the money. The dollars might not exactly have been rolling in yet, but at least Johnny now had a new career. They'd pile into that '54 Plymouth, put the bass fiddle on top and off they'd go, playing dates in and around Memphis. Places with names like Tootsie's Orchid Lounge and Junior's Dew Drop Inn and Pearl's Howdy Club.

While his recording career seemed to be finally heading in the right direction, Johnny's home life was not looking so healthy. Vivian was fed up of their never-ending financial problems. Johnny Cash genuinely wanted to provide for her, but he was earning a pittance and they lacked even the most basic necessities. It infuriated Vivian, who'd come from a family where hard work and all its rewards were taken for granted. But now she found herself married to a man who couldn't support his own wife. Now pregnant, Vivian also felt herself to be the odd one out with Johnny's friends. When she made herself a new maternity dress, she burst into tears because she thought it was too frumpy to wear with Johnny when he went on tour. In the end, Marshall's wife Etta had to talk the tearful Vivian into wearing the dress. Johnny was excited by the prospect of fatherhood, but also plagued by the worry that he couldn't earn the cash to keep a family. Pressure was building on the domestic front and he didn't know how to handle it.

On May 24, 1955, Vivian gave birth to a beautiful baby girl whom the couple called Rosanne. All along Johnny had been secretly praying for a boy, but straight after the birth he kissed his wife fervently and proclaimed, 'I don't care whether it's a boy or a girl, honey – just so we have a fine healthy baby!' Truth be told, however, Johnny had never felt so confused in all his life: on the one hand, he now had the family he had craved for so long, but at the same time he was dreading the future with them because he knew he couldn't support them.

Johnny was well aware of his new responsibilities. But, when he went home to their empty apartment the night his daughter was born, he found himself very worried. Except for a few dollars Vivian had in her purse at the hospital, they had perhaps twenty dollars in the whole world. Johnny concluded he only had himself as a potential source of revenue. He was going to have to make music pay the bills or else their lives – and marriage – would fall apart.

After Vivian came home from hospital, Johnny began staying up until the early hours writing new songs. He soon became frustrated, however, because Vivian wouldn't go to bed until he was ready. He wanted to create new songs but she'd wait up until he'd fallen asleep, with a burning cigarette usually still dangling from his mouth.

Johnny Cash and the Tennessee Two's first public appearance following the release of their record was as guest artists with singer Sonny James at a Saturday night country show in the armoury at Covington, Tennessee. They kicked off the set with their two recorded songs and were so well received that the audience called them back several times, to perform the same songs over and over again.

At another date shortly after this, Marshall suggested they sell photographs of Johnny. A photographer chum was enlisted to take the snaps and Johnny went down to a studio on Lamar Avenue and sat for a portrait. The snapper printed up fifty free prints for Marshall to test the market. At a show, in Arkansas, all fifty were unloaded at a quarter apiece. With a precedent set, another money-making aspect to their touring was established.

Throughout this period, Johnny Cash remained torn between supporting his family and getting his new-found career off the ground. 'Marshall had fond memories of those times,' he commented recently. 'But I don't. I don't really care to remember those first shows I played. It was new and exciting, but I knew there was something bigger ahead.

Those shows aren't pleasant memories. They're not the good old days.'

In the summer of 1955, Johnny performed his first major concert appearance as a guest on Elvis Presley's show at Overton Park Shell in Memphis. At the bottom of the advertisement in the Memphis *Press-Scimitar* that promoted Elvis's show was some very small print that read, 'Extra – Johnny Cash sings *Cry, Cry, Cry.*' He might have been getting only the smallest billing, but Johnny was happy; he had made it up there with the big boys. All Johnny's closest family and friends showed up for what was his first big official date of his career. The audience called him back and he did the newly recorded, but as yet unreleased, 'Folsom Prison Blues'.

Later, Johnny stood backstage and watched Elvis and felt stunned. It all seemed such a long way from the God-fearing folk of Dyess and those slow, sleepy Saturday afternoons fishing in a ditch. 'The audience reaction was always the same. The girls and women screamed, cried and fainted and, although the men would be jealous, nobody could keep them from watching him. He had a personal magnetism on- and offstage that was unique,' recalled Johnny many years later.

While in Memphis to see Sam Phillips, Johnny found himself with a few hours to kill before leaving the city, so he ducked into a movie theatre to pass the time. The film just happened to be *Inside the Walls of Folsom Prison*, and Johnny was instantly caught up in the tale of its primary character, a convict. Hours later he put pencil to paper and began crafting the lyrics to his latest song in less than an hour. After another hour, he had come up with the melody, and the following day he worked up the arrangement with

Perkins and Grant. Johnny recorded 'Folsom Prison Blues' in late 1955, but Sam Phillips judged it inappropriate for the Christmas season. He delayed its release until the following year, when it peaked at the number four position.

More than ten year later, the song re-emerged as an even bigger live recording and was labelled a country music classic. The release of that second single back in 1955 also enabled Johnny to finally quit his salesman job. He had now busted out on his own with his long hair and sideburns and the group's driving new sound had seen him dubbed everything from 'rockabilly' to 'white nigger'. Johnny regarded such comments with pride because in his eyes the people who made them were telling him he was different from everyone else. Johnny hadn't set out to sound different but, when he realised he *was* different, he was thrilled to death.

7

'I WALK THE LINE'

'Is Johnny Cash your real name?' Those were the words the legendary Carl Perkins uttered to Johnny Cash when they first met at Sun Records in late 1955. It marked the start of one of the longest and most enduring friendships in Johnny's life. Perkins reminded Johnny of his dearly departed brother Jack; Carl seemed filled with wisdom way beyond his years.

'I loved that "Cry, Cry, Cry",' Carl told Johnny. 'Let's do some shows together sometime.' Johnny and Carl played several dates together over the following few months. They had a lot of other things in common: Carl had been raised in the flat blacklands of West Tennessee, just across the river from Johnny's home in Arkansas. They were virtually the same age and seemed to have the same basic outlook on life. Carl looked set to be Johnny Cash's first true soulmate in the music industry.

On a hot day a few weeks later, soon-to-be megastar Elvis Presley walked into Sam Phillips's studio in Memphis, sat down at the piano and belted out 'Blueberry Hill' before starting to play a number of tuneful blues/gospel numbers. Then Elvis stopped, turned to his new friend Johnny and drawled, 'Let's sing some gospel.'

Johnny hesitated for a beat before looking at Elvis's kindly expression and realising this could be the opportunity of a lifetime. Johnny started humming gently and then found his place in the song that Elvis was hammering out on the piano. It turned out to be a magical music session, something that Johnny would never forget. They'd conjured up a unique harmony in the way that blew the staff at Sun Records away.

A few minutes later, Sam Phillips walked into the studio and introduced Johnny and Elvis to a guy he called 'a fantastic new talent' in the shape of an awkward country boy called Jerry Lee Lewis. Lewis immediately asked Elvis if he knew a classic gospel number written in 1907 entitled 'Will The Circle Be Unbroken', and Elvis nodded enthusiastically. So that day at Sun Records, a group of men including Johnny Cash, Elvis Presley, Jerry Lee Lewis and Carl Perkins sat around an upright piano and sang seven or eight gospel tunes. Producer Jack Clement taped that historic jam session, but kept it locked away in a bank vault somewhere in Memphis for more than thirty years.

Elvis, Carl, Jerry Lee and Johnny went on to sing ten more old hymn favourites and Elvis even stood up to allow Jerry Lee to sit at the piano for some of the tracks. The other three watched in awe as Jerry Lee came alive. None of them had ever seen a piano played like that before in their lives. Johnny made long-term friends with all three of those stars plus a host of other now legendary figures he came across at Sun Records. Elvis changed record labels shortly after their improvised singalong before eventually joining the Army. Johnny never saw much of him after that.

Another long-time friend Johnny met for the first time at Sun Records was Roy Orbison. He went on to work many tours with Roy, who later became his neighbour when he moved to Hendersonville, near Nashville. Orbison never forgot the generosity that Johnny showed him when tragedy befell him and his family many, many years later. Johnny in turn felt a special responsibility towards all of Orbison's family.

Johnny's new-found success was, to his mind, due to the spirited talent he was privileged to work with. He and his group were all of equal stature and there was rarely a show of jealousy between them. They helped each other, supported each other during concerts and shared all their successes with one another.

Backstage in Amory, Mississippi, just a few months after that historic get-together with those three superstar performers, Johnny Cash sat talking to his new friend Carl Perkins. He'd already performed, and Elvis was onstage. Johnny and Carl talked about the star-crazy audience and Johnny asked Carl why he didn't record more 'boppy' music. Carl said he'd love to, but hadn't yet come up with the right tune.

Then Johnny told his new friend a story about a black staff sergeant from Virginia named C V White, who had been stationed in Germany with him. White was always asking Johnny for reassurance that he was dressed right for a date or a night out. 'I'd always say, "Mighty spiffy, C V,"' recalled Johnny to Carl. 'Then he'd say, "Just don't step on my blue suede shoes, man," and he'd trip out the door snapping his fingers.'

Carl looked at his friend and after a moment spoke. 'That's a great idea for a 'bop' song!'

'That's why I told you,' insisted Johnny. 'With the feel you have for that kind of music, you're the man who should write it.'

Carl grabbed a pencil and a piece of brown paper bag and started writing. Before Elvis came offstage, he'd created 'Blue Suede Shoes'.

Musical history was being made by the talent from Sun Records. But Johnny Cash was living a Jekyll-and-Hyde existence. At work he was the tearaway musician with a fantastic future and a startling talent. But at home, he was treated as a 'waster' and 'non-provider' to his young family, who couldn't understand why he didn't get a 'proper' job like all the other husbands and fathers on the block where they lived. Johnny's pretty young wife Vivian knew only too well that her husband's frequent trips away from home would mark the beginning of the end of their marriage. Vivian's top priority was making a home and, as she watched the music world taking her man away from her, so she began to show less and less interest in it. Johnny insisted to Vivian that one day they would enjoy enormous wealth and fame beyond her wildest dreams. But she had to be patient. She took Johnny's words with a pinch of salt, unsure or unable to see anything beyond his frequent absences from the family.

The real money only began coming in when Johnny hit the

road as a live performer. By that time, Vivian was insisting on remaining at home most of the time, partly because she was not particularly interested in Johnny's musical career, but also because she was pregnant again. The marriage survived for the time being, but Vivian continued fighting against Johnny's career in every way possible. The harder the music business tried to pull Johnny away, the more she tried to pull him in the other direction.

Vivian was very afraid to be alone at their small apartment and even persuaded their friendly landlady to cut a door between their apartments so that Vivian could come and go when she wished. In turn, that made Johnny feel that life on the road was a lot more inviting than anything with his family.

Johnny and the Tennessee Two joined a country music package organised by Memphis DJ Bob Neal and began performing in auditoriums and ballrooms spread across the South, which meant hundreds of miles of monotonous driving. Johnny took along his green Plymouth because it was the newest car they had between them. In less than two years he piled over one hundred thousand miles on the mileometer. The first big tour travelled to Tupelo, Mississippi, and then back to Memphis, on a two-date gig. Elvis Presley and Johnny Cash and the Tennessee Two were the main support acts. The next tour pushed longer distance through Texas – Lubbock, Amarillo, Brownwood and San Angelo. Johnny's muddy, battered green Plymouth struggled to keep up with Elvis's flashy pink Cadillac as it chased across the flat Texas plains. The performers rendezvoused each night in a cramped dressing room with just enough time to tune up before rambling out on to the stage, plugging in their guitars and singing their hearts out. Often with the fans still applauding, they'd then climb back into their cars to drive through the night to the next day's date.

Johnny's trusted Plymouth rattled on to every stop even though the valves were burned out. Back in Memphis, Marshall and Luther sneaked the car into the back of the automobile sales shop for a complete overhaul and tune-up. They were so adept at such pit stops that they'd grind and replace the Plymouth's valves inside two hours. Johnny eventually saved up enough hard-earned cash to give the Plymouth to his father-in-law in San Antonio and purchase a faster maroon Lincoln from a local singer called Ferlin Huskie. The departure of that old vehicle marked the end of an era. It also meant the money was getting bigger – but then so were the problems.

The tours now reached east to Georgia and west to Colorado and Arizona. Johnny and the Tennessee Two made $50 a night on the road, then $75; finally, they topped $100. It was good money and it piled up, date after date. But all three still had to support three families plus the gas eaten up by the nonstop driving. Often they were forced to economise by finding a cheap motel with a double bed and single or rollaway. Once in the room they'd toss coins and the odd man out got his own bed, while the losers had to sleep together.

One bitterly cold winter night in Davenport, Iowa, Johnny and his two pals all crammed into a four-dollar motel room. Luther Perkins won the single rollaway bed. Before retiring, Johnny insisted on throwing open all the windows and even the door because of the stuffy heating system. When they awoke next morning, they found a small grey mouse lying half-frozen on the chilled floor. Marshall Grant turned up the radiator and as the steam started thumping, Johnny picked the mouse up by the tail and dangled it gingerly over the heat. Once the little animal began to stir, Johnny wrapped it in a tiny blanket made from a strip of cloth, and set the mouse on the warming radiator while they checked out.

Johnny and his friends tended to ignore the tattered 'Positively No Smoking' signs thumb-tacked to the back doors of many motel rooms. They also smuggled in hotplates and a skillet to cook up all sorts of meals. Back on the road, the threesome nibbled on cakes, crackers, sardines, pickles and chocolate bars. They even invested in a small portable grill and would pull up alongside the highway to barbecue steaks or pork chops. That was their main meal of the day. With no one in sight, Johnny and his pals even ate their meat without knives, forks and plates. A few years later, Johnny was still finding it mighty hard to kick that particular habit.

All three also packed their shotguns, convinced they could also live off the land. Whenever a likely target appeared, whoever was driving would hit the brakes and skid the car to a stop, doors would fly open and they'd all scramble out, shooting in every direction. One day, Johnny was driving through Alabama when he spotted a large bird on a farmhouse TV antenna. He stopped, jumped out and fired, eliminating not only the bird but the antenna too. As an angry farmer emerged from his house, Johnny jumped in the car and put his foot to the floor.

Back in Memphis, Johnny had played 'I Walk the Line' for Sam Phillips at Sun Records and he immediately agreed to record it. But, after several takes at the studios, Phillips insisted it should be sung faster. Johnny said it had been written as a slow ballad and refused to budge. Phillips begged his singing star to do just one more fast cut. Johnny reluctantly agreed, irritated that he'd let Phillips have the final say. The end result still had Johnny grizzling and Phillips went away promising to consider Johnny's request to only use the slow ballad version.

Six weeks later, Cash was driving home from a concert with group members Luther in the front and Marshall dozing in the back. About 1:00am they were listening to the *Opera Star Spotlight* on WSM from Nashville when DJ Eddie Hill said: 'We gotta new record by Johnny Cash and the Tennessee Two and we're gonna give it a spin.' It was 'I Walk the Line', but Sam Phillips's brisker, 'bootleg' version. Johnny was furious and smashed the dashboard with his fist. Marshall told him to call Phillips to insist he dropped it for his preferred cut. Next day, Cash angrily confronted Phillips, who shrugged his shoulders and told him not to worry.

'I Walk the Line' hit number 17 in the pop and number 2 in the country charts. Johnny earned enough from it to move his family out of their run-down apartment to a rented house, then on to their own property on Sandy Cove, in one of the best areas of Memphis.

The country music fan magazines now locked on to the newly acclaimed 'Man in Black'. *The Country Song Roundup* announced they 'really like this Cash fellow' and encouraged its readers to 'get those letters down to him. Remember this, every artist, no matter how big or small, loves to feel that his fans and record buyers are behind him one hundred per cent. It's up to you folks, so get those letters into us and we'll see that Johnny gets 'em.'

'I Walk the Line' turned out to be the pop music hit that gave Johnny true national recognition. Country music in the '50s, was still considered very local and few singers expected to get their names in the music trade magazines unless their record company had bought an advertisement. When 'I Walk the Line' topped the two million sales mark in the US, Johnny and the Tennessee Two were driving through North Carolina. Johnny was so delighted he suggested they celebrate by tucking into a bizarre local delicacy called snow cream. Local boy Marshall suggested they turn off the road and head up into the nearby mountains to find some snow. They eventually stopped in a place called Black Mountain, bought a dishpan, half a gallon of milk, a jar of vanilla flavouring, five pounds of sugar and a half-dozen eggs plus a huge mixing spoon. As dusk was falling they found a strip of snow on nearby Soco Mountain between the cities of Asheville and Cherokee, pulled their car over, got out and mixed themselves up some snow cream.

'It was about eleven o'clock when it was finally ready to eat,' Johnny explained many years later. 'And then, in the dark, we heard this bear a-huffing and a-puffing. We heard enough grunting out there to know what was coming. We left that whole dishpan of snow cream out there in the snow and jumped in the car and headed down that mountain.'

Tensions at home and the sheer boredom of life on the road probably contributed more than anything else to the hell-raising antics that Johnny came to be associated with at this time. Days and weeks constantly on the road until all dressing rooms and hotel lobbies began to look the same. Towns were memorable only for their audiences, and a performer's brief hour or so on stage was the only highlight of an otherwise tedious daily routine. That left Johnny and his pals to find their own diversions for the rest of the time.

The first disturbing habit came about when Johnny and his band started checking into hotel rooms and then breaking every stick of furniture in sight. Band member Chet Atkins was stunned when Johnny strolled into his room with a saw and sawed the legs off each table and chair. Then Cash called the front desk and asked for the manager to come to his room. He then castigated the starstruck fellow about the 'inferior quality of the furniture' – showing his handiwork as proof.

Trouble was, Johnny soon graduated to more dangerous behaviour, mainly thanks to Marshall Grant's reputation as a connoisseur of explosions. In the early days, they'd make firecrackers and set them off by the road as they sped along the highway. But those firecrackers grew in size and Marshall eventually began making them from black gunpowder and dynamite. They were more than capable of ripping apart a fat log and anything else that happened to be in its way.

Out on the road, band members began insisting on stopping at abandoned shacks where they'd plant sticks of dynamite underneath and then roar with laughter as these ramshackle buildings were blown sky high. It was all highly illegal, but in those early days Johnny's management chose to ignore the stunts because they saw the stunts as a harmless way for everyone to 'let off steam' during those arduous tours.

And Johnny Cash often joined in the 'fun'. He'd be sitting

in the back seat of their limo with a handmade bomb lying next to him and then insist to Marshall Grant in an excited voice, 'Marshall, we just gotta explode this damn thing otherwise I can't get no sleep back here!' The car would screech to a halt and they'd all creep out into the desert and explode their 'device' like a bunch of schoolkids.

Just before dawn one morning, Johnny and his pals pulled off to the side of a road near the New Mexico–Texas border. They walked out into the desert, set a bomb down and ran a trail of black powder from a five-pound keg all the way back to the roadside, before touching it off with a match. The makeshift fuse was laid long enough so that they were well out of sight before the explosion shook the ground. They turned around and drove back to survey the damage. At the site, a cluster of excited locals told them that a meteor had just hit the ground and exploded.

Carl Perkins later recalled how one of Marshall's bombs 'had enough powder to blow the car off the road' when it was set off near Tyler, Texas. Perkins said it also made the telephone wires sing for miles. Yet Marshall insisted he knew what he was doing. 'You wrap kite string tight around a five-keg of powder. The tighter you'd wrap it, the bigger the explosion it'd make. Sometimes we laid a stick of dynamite alongside.'

The group began leaving their shotguns at home and instead taking along a ten-gauge signal cannon that a friend had given to Marshall. Cash and his pals often loaded it with gravel and taped the charge with paper. On one chilly night in Minnesota, they decided to blow up a gaudy neon sign on a street corner. But, when the sign exploded, the recoil sent the cannon slamming into the right rear fender of Johnny's car. The cannon then bounced off and careened fifty yards down the road. Marshall retrieved the cannon and they all jumped into the car and careened up the street. That same cannon was also fired down hotel corridors late at night and taken backstage and used to mark one minute to go until the show began. But, compared to the activities that were just over the horizon, the cannon was positively small fry.

Back home, second daughter Kathleen was born on April 16, 1956, although much-travelled Johnny Cash rarely caught a glimpse of his newborn child as he rushed from venue to venue across the country.

When Johnny and his pals flew into Salinas, California, in 1956, at the invitation of a local promoter and country music fan called Stewart Carnall, it marked another major step towards nationwide recognition. The trio's first date was at the Big Barn, in Salinas, 'one of the roughest joints you'd ever seen in your life,' Carnall later recalled. 'But Johnny was as good then as he is now.' For the next ten days, Carnall chauffeured Cash and his boys around the circuit he'd booked in the central farmland of California.

The well-educated Californian promoter Carnall wasn't prepared for the rough-and-ready country boys from Tennessee, who spread fruit peelings all over the floor of his gleaming Cadillac El Dorado. They'd also insist on eating in what he later described as 'the worst goddamn joints'. And all three tended to eat meals with their bare hands because they couldn't be bothered to use a knife and fork.

Johnny and the Tennessee Two played two shows a night, which were separated by a country band hired by Carnall that played dance music. Johnny worked for a flat night's fee, which at first was $300 but then rose to $500, and finally $750; but out of that he had to pay his manager, Marshall, Luther and all the travel expenses. As Carnall later recalled, 'When we started, Johnny wasn't making enough to throw it away.'

When Johnny played The Louisiana Hayride, in Shreveport, Louisiana, it was the equivalent of The Grand Ole Opry in Nashville and the audience went wild for his latest songs such as 'Folsom Prison Blues'. Massive amounts of fan mail were also starting to trek to Johnny's door. Johnny would spread the letters out on the living-room floor of his house, counting the different states on the postmarks.

The Louisiana Hayride proved a brilliant springboard to success for many of the top country singers of the day including Faron Young, Webb Pierce, Hank Williams, George Jones and Johnny Horton, to name but a few. Cash knew this was also his route to greater fame and success and was delighted to become a regular at The Hayride and even agreed to be a featured guest every Saturday. But Johnny's regular stint at The Hayride marked another, less salubrious milestone: it was the first time he encountered a notorious breed of free-spirited females known to country entertainers as 'snuff queens'.

These women were probably the first real music world groupies to emerge as popular music took off in the late 1950s and they started showing up everywhere Johnny appeared. With dressing rooms overflowing with singers, musicians, their friends, fans, promoters and agents, it wasn't hard for the snuff queens to slip in unnoticed.

Some of Johnny's fellow musicians soon succumbed to temptation and disappeared arm-in-arm with the snuff queens. Johnny never admitted whether he was one of those takers, but he never tried to cover up the presence of such loose women. Stories about these free 'n' easy females being found sprawled drunkenly in the group's hotel suites soon spread across the country music world. But at least Johnny was still managing to resist the whisky and beer stacked up in every dressing room. He hadn't touched a drop since quitting the Air Force.

However the newly labelled Man in Black was feeling increasingly torn by his sky-rocketing success. Besides his neglected family he also felt guilty about not going to church. Johnny's tight touring schedule and late-night performances had all but killed off his ability to visit church. He'd failed in his obligations and was well aware of it. 'I didn't realise it then, but it was the beginning of a pattern, a working pattern which would stand for years,' Johnny later explained. 'My policy of aloneness and severed relationships from other committed Christians weakened me spiritually. Not that missing church necessarily meant missing God. It was just that Jesus never meant for us to try to make it on our own. There is something so important in worshipping together with other believers. And missing it left me vulnerable and easy prey for all the temptations and destructive vices that the backstages of the entertainment world had to offer.'

Temptations meant that ever-present demon, deception, was once more lurking just around the corner.

8

THE DEMON DECEPTION

Johnny Cash's newly found star status had a serious effect on his relationships with friends, acquaintances and people he'd known all his adult life. He saw himself as the same man; they now saw him as a very different person from the humble country boy of earlier. It was a deeply frustrating experience for the singer that ate away at him constantly.

Johnny wanted his old relationships to remain the same. But few of his former friends would allow that, and their attitude towards him changed. He felt they didn't trust him any more; they saw him as some big-time show-off who had no time for common folk like them. The easy give-and-take that had always marked their get-togethers became virtually impossible, except for a handful of Johnny's closest friends who knew him the best and were nothing but happy for his success. It was almost as if everyone expected him to be different because he'd become rich and famous. They assumed that difference had arisen, despite everything he did to persuade them it didn't exist.

In 1957, Johnny quit his regular gig at The Louisiana Hayride for Nashville's prestigious Grand Ole Opry, taking a hefty pay cut in the process. Johnny still toured in the week and then missed the most lucrative personal appearance night on the road on Saturdays because he was contracted to be back in Nashville for the Opry. He sang Saturday nights in Nashville as a regular for a year, making a very modest salary, and then quit. It was a typical Johnny Cash move: he'd fast become a hot property on the country music circuit, but he wanted to stay very much in control of his own destiny.

Stewart Carnall picked up on Johnny's attitude and also, naturally, recognised his huge earning potential. He worked out a deal that allowed him to buy into half of Johnny's existing contract for $5,000 and seven per cent of the singer's gross for the following year. The first thing Carnall did was book Johnny on a nightly minimum guarantee, which was then applied against a percentage of the box-office takings for all his appearances.

With Carnall handling him, Johnny began spending more time in California, which meant even more hours of travelling from city to city. So it wasn't that surprising when his career took a definite step in the wrong direction. Johnny was touring with Grand Ole Opry artists Ferlin Husky and Faron Young, when he became close friends with a man called Gordon Terry, who worked with Faron. One night, the group of them were driving in two cars to Jacksonville, Florida, following a concert in Miami. Everyone was clearly shattered and Gordon – who was driving Faron's limousine – pulled over and stopped. Johnny's party stopped behind him. Everyone got out of the cars to stretch their legs and Gordon walked over to Luther, who was driving Johnny's car.

'You sleepy, Luther?' Gordon asked.

'Sure am,' came the reply.

Then a friend offered Luther a small white pill with a cross on it. He called it a 'bennie' and promised it would help his friend to 'enjoy' himself once the group of entertainers got to Jacksonville. Johnny Cash was also offered a pill by the friend and accepted it. Within thirty minutes, he was chatting away and feeling refreshed and wide awake. That night in Jacksonville, Johnny took more pills and did the show feeling great. Johnny believed he'd discovered something that was good for him. He couldn't have been more wrong.

Johnny was convinced the pills could pep him up and make him really feel like doing a show. The pills came in a variety of shapes and sizes and they had already become popular with truck drivers, who used them to stay awake on long hauls across the country. Then came amphetamines, Dexedrine, Benzedrine and Dexamyl. A cocktail of stimulants awaited newly crowned young star Johnny Cash. Johnny soon discovered there was one very special black pill that was so strong it 'would take you all the way to California and back in a '53 Cadillac with no sleep', according to one associate.

For the first couple of years of regular drug-taking, Johnny reckoned he discovered newly expanded limits to his own stamina and performing ability. He'd always loved performing, but had suffered constantly from 'butterflies'. Once he swallowed back a couple of those pills, he felt a burst of self-confidence running through his body and seemed invincible.

The most chilling aspect of Johnny's addiction to 'poppers' was that they were so easy to get hold of. He'd simply phone a physician out of the Yellow Pages, tell him who he was and even openly admit, 'I need some of those diet pills to keep me awake.' Within minutes he'd have a bottleful clasped in the palm of his hand.

Eventually he'd start asking for larger-sized pills, and more of them. Johnny was well and truly hooked and he had no one to turn to. He didn't even recognise the dangers himself. As he later recalled, 'Sometimes I'd get so high, I'd be above my conscience, but when I came down it would still be there. From time to time I'd worry a bit that the pills were beginning to hurt me, but I'd take another pill and I wouldn't worry any more.'

Inevitably, Johnny began starting to experience difficulties remembering his lines when he sang and would fluff interviews with journalists. It wasn't long before it began to dawn on him that maybe the pills were the cause. Everyone around Johnny was starting to notice the change in his character. In the past, his pals had always made a joke out of his nervousness – a serious twitch in his neck, back and face; his eyes dilating; an inability to stand still; his habit of constantly twisting, turning, contorting and popping his neck bones. Johnny later recalled: 'It sometimes felt like someone had a fist between my shoulder blades, twistin' the muscle and bone, stretchin' my nerves, torturing 'em to breakin' point.'

Back home, wife Vivian had no idea the drugs had taken hold of her husband. On Johnny's rare visits to his family, he'd often awaken in the middle of the night and walk around the house in a desperate attempt to try and wear out the effect of the pills. Other times, he'd wake the entire household by taking off in his car for hours through the nearby streets until he either wrecked it or finally slumped to a halt from exhaustion.

Perhaps surprisingly, there was one unexpectedly positive side to the endless hours Johnny spent travelling down nameless, dark highways on tour. His songwriting was becoming more and more inspired by the boredom of life on the road. Johnny's pockets were constantly overflowing with scraps of paper covered in poems that would eventually become lyrics for his songs. Johnny taught himself the knack of outlining a song with random guitar chords and runs, jotting key words or entire verses on whatever scrap of paper was handy at that moment in time. He'd pull out those pieces of paper, often weeks later, and add a bit more until he'd completed it. Johnny Cash wrote more than five hundred songs this way during his lifetime.

With his popularity soaring by the week, the Man in Black had less and less time for his family and life at home. He didn't often phone Vivian because he couldn't face talking to her when he was out of his head on pills. On tour, the only way he could keep awake was to swallow back handfuls of amphetamines and barbiturates. And the demon drink was also beckoning. He began getting completely smashed on a lethal cocktail of liquor and, often, even cannabis.

These appalling excesses meant Johnny's voice was often no more than a mere whisper, although audiences still found his lyrics inspiring – and intimidating. His success was now translating to the national stage, with regular big television appearances, including spots on Dick Clark's *American Bandstand*, *The Ed Sullivan Show* and shows hosted by Jackie Gleason and Lawrence Welk. Johnny also popped up regularly on Red Foley's *Ozark Jubilee*.

Johnny was performing in every state in the country. Then came tours across Canada and into Europe and even the Far East. And wherever Johnny was – be it the London Palladium, Carnegie Hall, the Hollywood Bowl or Pine Bluff, Arkansas – he always sang 'I Walk the Line'.

Back home, Vivian gave birth to the couple's third child – another daughter, Cindy – on July 29, 1958. Vivian didn't really have time to worry much about Johnny or his strange, pill-induced behaviour – she had three little children to cope with. In many ways, it was better when Johnny was out of her hair. His parenting skills left a lot to be desired.

Johnny split from Sun Records in late 1958, claiming that he needed to be better marketed to mainstream audiences across the globe. Sam Phillips ensured the split was amicable and Cash signed with Columbia Records, who released two albums in the first year – *The Fabulous Johnny Cash* (a title that Johnny found very embarrassing) and an album of gospel and religious songs.

The move to Columbia had been cleverly manipulated following a meeting between Johnny and Don Law, a veteran A&R man, who controlled a number of well-known country artists at Columbia. British-born Law was emerging as one of the true pioneers of the American recording industry. When he first started in the business in Dallas, he later explained: 'We recorded on waxes that we had to preheat, and we couldn't play them back so we didn't know what we had. To keep the street noises out, we had to keep the windows closed, so we worked shirtless with electric fans blowing across cakes of ice. We recorded in hotel rooms and we'd put the bass player and drummer in the bathroom.' The advent of the acetate disk in the mid-1930s certainly made recording a much easier process.

Law was intrigued by Johnny Cash and convinced he was on the verge of superstardom: 'He was totally different from anybody I ever recorded. He was an excellent writer, but his mind was always open to other good writers. He'd do anybody else's material if he felt it was right for him.'

Initially, Law convinced Johnny to hold a recording session in Hollywood, at a small studio off the infamous Sunset Boulevard. When Johnny suggested performing with a big band, Law discouraged him because he didn't want to 'water down' what he perceived as Johnny's biggest strength – his directness and simplicity. As Law later explained: 'It's a virility and a guts to his voice that he's got. He's always sung off pitch, but he can just walk out and say, "I'm Johnny Cash."'

At the end of 1958, Johnny and Vivian bought a brand new home in Walnut Grove, Memphis, with their new-found riches. Johnny wasn't entirely happy at the move, however, because he felt they didn't spend enough time in the city to be based there. The house was quickly sold and promoter Stewart Carnall persuaded Johnny to move to his home state of California – a land of opportunities for a man with his talent and ambition.

Johnny drove Vivian and daughters Rosanne, Kathy and

Cindy all the way to Los Angeles. Initially, they lived in an apartment hotel in the shabby area of North Hollywood, where baby Cindy slept in one of the drawers of a cupboard. Vivian found it lonely and miserable because she didn't even own her own property. The streets of North Hollywood seemed filthy and littered with life's failures and she was determined not to be dragged down to their level. She started to question her husband's relentless quest for worldwide fame. Was it really worth all these sacrifices?

In 1959, Johnny Cash and the Tennessee Two started playing benefit concerts at prisons after Johnny made it clear he wanted to put something back into society. The first date was a low-profile gig at Texas State Prison, in Huntsville, during a downpour of rain. But they stayed out there, playing in the middle of a rodeo arena with prisoners all around them, and not one of the cons tried to get out of the rain.

Johnny and his two pals got the same reaction at all the prisons they subsequently visited. These included Cummins, in Arkansas, Hutchinson, in Kansas, the infamous Folsom and San Quentin, California. They played San Quentin when Merle Haggard was a prisoner there. Johnny Cash spoke to Haggard, who later said Johnny had been an inspiration to him. Johnny believed that prisoners and servicemen made the best audiences for him because they were genuinely responsive. He also felt a bond with them. He knew how to talk to them and never *talked down* to them.

In 1959, Johnny tried to appease his wife by purchasing legendary US entertainer Johnny Carson's vast house in Encino, near Los Angeles, for his family for $75,000 (£50,000). It was expensive, but Johnny could afford it now.

He'd sold over six million records in the first four years of his career.

The Tennessee Two – Marshall and Luther – both agreed to move out to Hollywood as well, although they didn't like it and moved back to Memphis within a year. None of that really mattered, because the group was travelling so much they didn't have to live near each other. Instead, they'd simply rendezvous at the first date of each tour.

Johnny quickly adjusted to the southern Californian lifestyle, which perfectly camouflaged him from his inner turmoil fuelled by increasing amounts of drugs and drink. Hollywood was the ideal 'candy store' for Johnny Cash. Whatever he wanted he got. His nights were filled with clubs, supposedly important friends and adoring fans. Even Hollywood producers started approaching him to consider movie roles.

Back on the musical front, however, Johnny could do no wrong. He was in the country music fast lane. In the middle of 1959, one ten-day tour through Canada and the Midwest grossed more than $70,000. All his shows were sell-outs several weeks in advance.

With America virtually conquered, Johnny made his first major tour overseas, to Australia, where his records were selling like hotcakes. Johnny appeared at the Sydney stadium in a 'fire-engine-red' sports jacket with a black shirt and red flowers, powder-blue slacks and white pumps. An audience of almost twenty thousand that night and thirty thousand the following evening gave him standing ovations at both shows. It was the largest crowd he'd ever played to up until then. Much larger crowds would eventually follow. Johnny's personal earning that year – 1959 – topped a quarter of a million dollars.

He also made recording history by becoming the first composer-performer of country & western music whose every record release during a four-year period (1956–59) reached the top ten of the *Billboard* charts. 'I Walk the Line', 'Next in Line', 'You're the Nearest Thing to Heaven' and 'Big River' to name but a few. 'I Walk the Line' was, and still is, Johnny's hit of hits as it harked back to his unhappy experiences as that unsuccessful door-to-door salesman before he hit the big time. The title was actually borrowed in 1960 for a movie starring Gregory Peck, and Johnny ended up singing his own ballads as background music.

'Five Feet High and Risin", 'Luther Played the Boogie' and 'The Man in the Hill' were the main releases in 1959. There was no stopping Johnny Cash now, just so long as he could keep the rest of his life under control.

9

'LITTLE JEWELS'

On the road, the wisecracks and pranks continued despite all the drugs, drinks and chaos. It seemed the easiest way for Johnny Cash to cope with his success was to pretend that it hadn't happened and continue behaving exactly the same way he always had. He undoubtedly wanted to cling to the old ways, trying to deny that financial success made life any more enjoyable. Johnny began hiding behind a string of practical jokes that steadily escalated in intensity and destructiveness.

A classic Johnny-style prank involved him rousing Stewart Carnall from a sleep in the back of their limo by tossing a lit-up string of between eighty and a hundred tiny firecrackers in his lap. Another time, Johnny went fishing during a day out while appearing in a one-week run at the Showboat, in Las Vegas. Early that evening he rolled in with fifteen fat trout, cleaned them in his hotel room and saved the heads, tails and entrails, which he then slipped between Marshall Grant's bottom sheet and his mattress – an act that did nothing to improve their already fractious friendship.

Luther Perkins was undoubtedly the low-key member of the trio. He was homesick for Memphis. Moreover, Luther insisted on taking a nap every afternoon before all evening performances. Marshall and Johnny took great delight in waiting until he fell asleep before leaning across and carefully setting Luther's watch two or three hours ahead so he'd wake up at seven thinking it was nine and that he was late for the show.

In Grand Rapids, Michigan ('one of our wilder towns', according to Stewart Carnall), Johnny insisted on Gordon Terry waiting the entire evening in an all-night coffee shop near the hotel. Johnny then walked in with Marshall's pistol under his coat, and appeared to start an argument with Terry. With all the customers watching, Johnny pulled out the weapon and fired a shot towards Terry, who smashed a capsule of catsup under his shirt and collapsed on the floor. Johnny stuck the pistol in his belt, turned and swaggered out the door. Two fans from that night's show looked on in astonishment, but didn't dare utter a word.

Other stunts included dropping balloons filled with water from hotel rooms on to unsuspecting passers-by. In Niagara Falls – with temperatures dipping under thirty degrees below freezing at the time – Cash and his pals poured water from wastebaskets down on to arriving guests. Eggs and more water followed all through the afternoon. They almost got slung in jail. Another favourite stunt was to check into a hotel and hand the bellhop a small suitcase full of lead curtain weights – weighing more than a hundred pounds. Such pranks may have broken up the tedious aspects of touring but they weren't exactly endearing Johnny and his pals to those members of his supposedly beloved public that he came across.

A few harmless jokes had escalated into something that was threatening real trouble. Johnny and his gang would throw lamps out of windows on arrival in new motels just to hear the sound of them breaking. In one hotel, they filled the bathtub with hot water and emptied a case of Jello (jelly) into it before checking out. In another, they stuck hamburgers, cheese and sardines into the indirect lighting in the elevator, which proved incredibly foul smelling. They also made what Marshall Grant later called 'goms' – lumps of mayonnaise, cheese, sardines and mustard – which were then left on hotel radiators or in elevators.

In Iowa, Johnny and his boys smuggled two hundred feet of rope into a hotel room. That night, on hands and knees, they tied the doors of every room on the seventh floor together, kicked the doors to wake the sleeping guests and crawled back into their rooms. The management eventually released the frantic occupants.

Years later, Johnny admitted all these ludicrous excesses by explaining, 'I've always had a bad streak of vandalism in me. Let's face it. I really have. In Dyess, I used to go out and break bottles and run. I had a buddy and we'd go into a farmer's field at night and burn the haystack down. I'd never think of doin' this alone. But, put me with this mean buddy of mine, and I'd do anythin'.'

The key to Johnny's behaviour was how easily he was influenced by others. He'd never have started taking pills if they hadn't been offered; he'd never have started exploding things if Marshall hadn't taught him how. There was a streak of weakness running through Johnny Cash that might yet prove his downfall. As the stunts escalated, so did the damage Johnny and his pals were inflicting. In one motel in Georgia, the group asked for adjoining rooms but when they found there were no connecting doors they grabbed a fire axe from the hallway and chopped their own entrance way.

Usually, the group's irresponsible offstage antics didn't continue onstage. But on New Year's Eve 1956, in New Jersey, the two worlds finally met. Marshall – by now nicknamed 'The Mad Bomber' by many of their entourage – was handed a cherry bomb in the dressing room. He lit it, tossed it into the toilet and flushed it. As he later recalled: 'I stood there for about sixty seconds. Then soundlessly the pipes came off the wall and the commode shattered.'

The police were called and Johnny told them that a small boy with an axe had knocked the pipes off the wall and chopped up the commode, adding that he had last been seen disappearing down the hallway. When the police left, the group went upstairs to see what damage had been inflicted on the nearest public lavatories. As Marshall later explained: 'There were about twenty-five people wiping themselves off. The contents of the toilets had exploded all over the room.'

The trio continued to thrash their cars severely. One time, they built a campfire in the back of a rented station wagon. They were so hard-wearing on one car they had in California that, 'there were dents in there that you could lay a sack of feed in,' according to one member of the entourage. The cost of all this vandalism was running into the thousands for every tour. In Germany, in November, 1960, Johnny flung his Bowie knife at a *Mona Lisa* reproduction painting hanging on the wall of his hotel room. Johnny openly admitted later: 'I was goin' through the lobby, and some drunken German called me an American pig. I should have whipped him. But I got mad and took it out on the picture instead.' He was charged a thousand dollars for that particular incident.

Not surprisingly, word of Johnny's outrageous behaviour was getting round the country music business. Some groups tried to emulate the trio's outrageous antics and the group were regularly blamed for damage they hadn't actually caused. Many were appalled by their apparent indifference to other people's possessions.

Incredibly, virtually none of these incidents received any public exposure. Some believe that, if Johnny had been 'nailed' earlier on, then he might not have continued taking more and more uppers and downers to fuel his excessive lifestyle, which by now was careering completely out of control. Negative publicity might have sparked closer scrutiny of Johnny and his entourage, which would have opened up some wounds but possibly also forced them to curb their more extreme antics.

Johnny never revealed what drove him to pop ever-increasing numbers of pills. He did once claim that the death of Texan country singer Johnny Horton in 1960 helped push him further into the hands of what he subsequently referred to as the 'demon deception'. Horton had recorded a succession of lively historical broadcasts, the most successful being 'Battle of New Orleans'. On November 5, 1960, he died in a head-on automobile collision just outside Milano, Texas. Johnny had been attending a disc jockey convention in Nashville when he heard about Horton's death. He left immediately to help bring the body back from Texas and delivered the eulogy over the casket at the funeral; Don Law was one of the pallbearers. Years later, however, he admitted: 'I acted like it upset me, but it didn't really. I acted weird about his death, but it was pills I was on that made me weird about it.'

There was another death that still lingered as freshly in his mind as if it had only just happened – that of his brother Jack. Having risen to the top of country music, with thousands of shows and millions of records already behind him, Johnny found himself no more at peace than all those years earlier. 'I think it was the miserable streak in me. Maybe I was afraid to face reality then. I wasn't very happy then. Maybe I was trying to find a spiritual satisfaction in drugs,' he mused many years later. 'It was an escape, that's all. When I first started, pills made me feel good. Every time I took them, I felt good. Then I took so many that I just didn't feel good. I was only awake.' And the memories of Jack continued to haunt him.

In 1960, Johnny Cash finally succumbed to the attractions of the lucrative nightclub circuit, although that didn't stop him hating every minute of it. He later said he felt uncomfortable in nightclubs because the audiences there were much harder to please. They didn't automatically applaud his every note and sometimes they could even get rather nasty. Johnny later complained, 'We weren't big enough at that time, and they wouldn't pay any real attention to us. They were too busy drinkin'.'

During a series of live appearances in Syracuse, New York and Atlantic City, Johnny took along a young drummer, named W S Holland, for musical back-up. He worked out so well that Holland eventually joined the Tennessee Two, which then – logically enough – became the Tennessee Three. Everyone called the blond, husky-voiced young man 'Fluke'. He'd been an air-conditioning repairman in Jackson, Tennessee, but played clubs at night. Johnny had heard of Fluke through Carl Perkins and, within minutes of his first appearance with Johnny, Fluke's appointment was rubber stamped.

'Guess you wanna know how much money you're gonna make?' Johnny asked the young drummer.

'Nope,' came the reply. 'Enough for a few groceries'll be fine.'

'You wanna work for me occasionally?' asked the puzzled Man in Black.

'Nope, need a steady job,' came Fluke's razor-sharp reply.

'I mean,' explained Johnny. 'D'you wanna work whenever I work?'

'That'd be good.'

Johnny then told Fluke how much he'd be paid. But he never got that amount – Johnny always paid him even more.

• • • •

In California, Johnny and Stewart Carnall bought a racehorse together after chartering a plane to go down to a yearling sale in Del Mar. They splashed out $2,100 on the last horse on sale at the auction and named him 'Walk The Line'. Ironically, however – considering its name – the horse went lame almost immediately and they had to have his legs blistered. Then he limped so badly during training at Santa Anita, they had to pull him out of his first race. 'He was a financial disaster,' Carnall admitted years later. 'The trainer had to put his legs in ice packs so he could run a course.'

With Vivian and the kids firmly entrenched in Encino, California, Johnny immersed himself still further in the Hollywood lifestyle. He later admitted he enjoyed cruising Sunset Strip looking at the slinky hookers touting their bodies on the kerbside, though he insisted he never fell for their sleazy charms. Other temptations proved harder to turn down. Johnny still couldn't resist occasionally stage managing a bit of drama on his quieter days. Stewart Carnall explained: 'We'd have somebody sittin' on a bench on Hollywood Boulevard and we'd drive up and three of us in black suits and hats would jump out and drag him bodily into the car and drive off. People would just watch and never holler.'

By this time, Johnny owned a number of cars including a flashy 1932 Plymouth roadster, which he'd painted a knotty pine to match his kids' den at home. He called the automobile 'Ole Crop Failure'. One time, Johnny and Gordon Terry dragged singer Warren Smith downtown in the car after tying him up and gagging him. Johnny later explained: 'Gordon had a Colt .45 and a shotgun and I had my pistol and a Winchester rifle. We rode up and down Hollywood Boulevard with Warren and then stopped in front of the Security First National Bank with all these guns stickin' out. And some guy walked up to us and asked us how to get to Hollywood and Vine.'

Another time, Carnall gave Johnny a brand new three-piece set of expensive leather luggage. Johnny was over the moon. Unfortunately, during a fast check-out from a Buffalo hotel, he threw all the luggage out of the bedroom window. When he retrieved it on the ground, the locks were split. Carnall later recalled: 'Johnny thought it was hilarious and used the luggage for a year with wire and rope wrapped around it. He'd pack at the last minute by grabbing wads of clothes and shoving them into the cases. We'd never get to the airport more than ten minutes before a flight. If we arrived before that, he'd drive around the airport. He knew I'd always stop the plane.'

Johnny was usually paid his fee in cash after each show and would often come home to Vivian and the kids with wads of notes literally spilling out of his pockets. He never seemed to have time to go to the bank. Carnall recalled $7,100 sitting in an old jar for several weeks before Johnny finally took it to the bank. Often, his daughters would play with the money on the kitchen floor. Sometimes, it'd end up in the washing machine.

Down at a local market in Encino one day, Johnny tried to write a cheque for some groceries. His records were on sale in the store, but the manager wouldn't accept the cheque, and Johnny didn't have any cash. Eventually he rushed home, rummaged around in the house for what he could find and carried a paper bag of cash back to the market. He dumped it out on the check-out counter with the words, 'Take out what you need.' The sack held $16,000.

Johnny's biggest weakness in life was that he'd always try anything once. It had led him down that destructive path to drink and drugs. Now his openness to new experiences landed him with a lead role in a project dubiously entitled *Five Minutes To Live*. Johnny played a maniacal killer in what can only be described as a poorly scripted B-thriller. (The title song, which he performed, bore the memorable title 'I've Come To Kill'!) At the time, however, Johnny assured showbusiness reporters: 'It's gonna be a good 'un. My leadin' lady – I forget her name – and I, have some good scenes.' Oh dear …

The billboards promoted Johnny as 'a lusty, romantic, guitar singing [sic] powerhouse', but the film was appalling. After its short-lived release, Johnny admitted he'd made a terrible mistake and later said of the movie (which was recut and released again in the mid-Sixties as *Door To Door Maniac*), 'I shouldn't have done it. My leadin' lady was the producer's wife.' To many cynics, it sounded like a typical Tinseltown tale.

Johnny also began adding to his gun collection around this time. Often he'd buy half a dozen new weapons at any one time. He'd been a fine marksman back in Arkansas, as had his father, and guns genuinely fascinated him. He even practised fast-draw and hand-loading his own cartridges. Guns gave Johnny a sense of security although they sometimes worried those around him.

Around this time, Johnny bought an entire trailer park near Ojai, California, so he could get his parents to move from Memphis. They wound up agreeing to run the trailer park for him. The first fifteen trailers to settle in the new Johnny Cash Trailer Rancho received free Cash records.

Johnny adored the arid mountain region north of his home in Encino so much that he decided the family should head further north. In Casitas Springs, a small valley northwest of Ventura, he purchased fifteen steep hillside acres and had a rambling five-bedroom ranchhouse built, which was completed in late 1961. Johnny later said he felt much more at home in Casitas Springs. He loved walking the brown hills and going out shooting in his back yard. Johnny even opened an office on Ventura's main street and insisted that onetime promoter and now personal manager Carnall join him up there. But Carnall wasn't keen on leaving Los Angeles and subsequently their business relationship started to fall apart. The situation wasn't helped by the fact that Carnall also discovered his star performer was dabbling even more heavily than before in pep pills. 'He'd changed from the person I enjoyed being with to a person who was brooding and moody when the pills got hold of him,' explained Carnall years later.

In July, 1961, Carnall 'sold' Johnny to a Canadian promoter called Saul Holiff, for a tour through Newfoundland and Nova Scotia. It was the last tour connected to Carnall. He parted with Johnny soon afterwards following an acrimonious phone conversation. Neither ever fully explained what had happened.

Saul Holiff was a very different type of manager to Stew Carnall. Holiff was renowned for regularly carrying around enormous sums of cash in a suitcase just in case he had to buy himself – or his client – out of trouble. In many ways, Holiff was as much of a showman as Johnny. Soon he'd also taken over management of Carl Perkins, The Statler Brothers and The Carter Family, along with numerous Canadian stars.

Holiff quickly learned not to let his own huge ego take over the limelight from his most valuable commodity – Johnny Cash. He cleverly played down his relationship with the star, something which appealed to Johnny. One of Holiff's favourite phrases was: 'Here I am, an urban Canadian Jew managing a rural American Baptist.'

Some of Johnny's pals sniped at Holiff, sniffing that he lived across the border for tax purposes, but Johnny took no notice of the gossips just so long as the money kept rolling in. The two men certainly had their problems – splitting up in 1963, 1966, 1967 and 1968 – but they came back together again and again. Holiff always affirmed his loyalty to Johnny by having a floor-to-ceiling blow-up photo of the singer in concert dominating his main Ontario office. Holiff was renowned as one of the best managers in the business because he astutely knew what *not* to do.

That didn't stop Holiff having a taste for the good things in life, such as the best hotels, best limos, best food and wines. Johnny, on the other hand, didn't really give a damn about such things. Holiff had to stop staying at the exclusive Essex House hotel, on Central Park West, New York City, after Johnny washed down the third floor with a firehose during yet another reckless night on a pill-popping spree. That night Holiff found Johnny's trousers on the fifth floor of the hotel and had them taken down and put in a safety deposit box. Then he got a receipt to make sure Johnny didn't think his money had been taken. As Holiff later explained: 'Johnny could be half-dead and still notice everythin'.'

Not all the problems were so easily managed. Holiff

refused to crawl and ingratiate himself to Cash when he was drugged off his head. Sometimes, Johnny exploded at Holiff who'd shout back. Next day, it was always Johnny who came crawling back pleading forgiveness from his manager. As Holiff later explained: 'I'm very proud of one thing. I've never crawled over anybody. In a business where you crawl or step over everybody, I've never had to do it. I'm the antithesis of what I should be in this damn business.'

Holiff's tough-guy stance didn't stop Johnny making him a victim of some appallingly childish pranks. One time, in a small restaurant in Canada, Marshall ordered a large wedge of banana pie with thick meringue. Johnny and Gordon Terry anticipated what was coming and slid off their stools towards the kitchens. A few minutes later the pie was set in front of Holiff by group member Marshall, who slammed it down so hard on the table that bits of banana filling and meringue splattered all over Holiff. The promoter/manager jumped up and looked around with indignation, but no one reacted so he sat down again, cleaning himself off. Even he had to turn a blind eye to the Cash pranks sometimes. Not long afterwards there was another incident in which Johnny threw three more banana pies at Holiff as he was driving a car alongside a limo carrying Johnny and his trio of band members. It seemed to many that Johnny was trying to push his manager to the limits of his tolerance.

• • • •

'This is a hard life. The secret is: go when you gotta go; sleep when you can; eat when you can. It's that simple. You can go on thataway. If you don't get the right kind of food and the right kind of rest, you can't do it. That's why they take the pills.' Johnny's drummer Fluke Holland had it just about right when he said those words; Johnny's addiction to pills was threatening to destroy his life. For, behind the gruelling touring schedules and nonstop personal appearances, Johnny was now succumbing to depression following the long periods of drug-induced highs. He was burdened with guilt about his absences from his family and desperately prayed for the strength to fight the drug habits that were threatening to take complete control of his unstructured life.

As Fluke Holland later explained: 'If you're in Nashville and have to be in Dallas tomorrow night, it's real easy to take a pill to get you there. But then you'll get there and, instead of sleeping, you'll stay up and take another one and then you get to the show and take one to do the show. Then you might want to go to a club and roar afterwards, and you'll take another one and stay up half the night. Then you'll go to bed and feel so terrible when you wake up that you'll take another one. It's the way 90 per cent of them start on pills.' The pressures were inevitable; some days the group travelled seven or eight hundred miles. One night it might be Phoenix then it was on to San Francisco the next and most of it was by car. Added Fluke, 'It's so expensive to fly. That's what gets them on the pills.'

By the early Sixties, Johnny Cash reckoned he was giving 290 shows annually over a circuit of three hundred thousand miles. The audiences averaged at least three thousand people for each performance, which meant he was singing to nearly a million people a year. And when he wasn't out performing he was making records for Columbia. There was no break and as the strain mounted so did his intake of drugs, especially amphetamines.

Johnny Cash faced internal as well as external pressures. His newly acquired self-confidence was eroding as the lows gradually took over from the highs. He was once again finding it frightening to walk out and perform before any crowd. The real Man in Black was diffident, retiring and somewhat moody. He was also never completely comfortable with strangers, despite his popularity.

At first, the pills hadn't been supplemented with alcohol as Johnny was not a big drinker, but by 1962, according to one associate, Johnny was willing to down a pint of vodka as a dare. At another stage Johnny quit drink altogether initially and increased his intake of pills as a 'replacement' for all that missing alcohol. Then he went back on both.

Pill popping was an accepted practice among many country music artists. One of the greatest stars, Hank Williams, had died from an overdose of barbiturates on the way to a date in Canton, Ohio. He was just 29 years old at the time. A lot of folk could see similarities between him and Johnny, who by now was exactly the same age Hank Williams had been when he died.

These drugs were so commonly used they were given secret nicknames by the hardened users. Years later Johnny explained: 'There's the "old yellers". That's plain Dexedrine. There's "little jewels". That's a name for just any of them. And there's "popcorn" time capsules that pop every two and a half hours or so.' And so it went on.

An appearance on the American TV programme *The*

Mike Wallace Show revealed the damage that drugs had already done to Johnny Cash. He knew that many people in the media were aware of his narcotics habit and feared that his twitchiness, dry mouth and dilated eyes would give away his condition. As a reaction to his inner fears, Cash glared at Wallace from the moment he was introduced to the programme's tens of millions of viewers across America.

'Do you really like showbusiness?' asked Wallace pointedly.

'It beats pickin' cotton,' Johnny shot back.

'What else did you do in Arkansas besides picking cotton,' Wallace enquired.

'I killed snakes,' Johnny continued on the war path.

'You look a bit snaky yourself,' observed Wallace.

'Watch out I don't strike you,' Johnny snapped back.

Wallace then tried to change the subject – he sensed there was a real danger of a physical clash on-screen.

'Why are you bringing country music to Carnegie Hall?' he asked.

'Why not?' Johnny growled back.

The interview was then ended abruptly by the show's producer.

The drying agent in the amphetamines, along with the cigarettes and alcohol, sparked chronic bouts of laryngitis for Johnny. It sometimes lasted for days, even weeks. One night, Johnny's voice was so shot to pieces he could barely whisper. His supporting acts, The Carter Family, Tompall and the Glaser Brothers, and Merle Kilgore, all saved the evening for him. The audience was bitterly disappointed by Johnny's pathetic performance that night, although they accepted the MC's explanation that he had a bad cold and laryngitis.

Afterwards, Johnny found a dark corner backstage and slumped into a dark depression. At one point in the evening, Maybelle Carter and her daughters Helen, Anita and June came back to try and cheer him up. It was an uphill task.

June Carter immediately recognised the symptoms of excessive drug use as she looked into Johnny's dilated pupils. He turned away nervously, painfully aware of her. As he walked away, she called after him, 'We were praying for you out there tonight.'

'I am afraid I wasn't praying with you,' whispered a gaunt-looking Johnny. He needed more than prayers alone to help sort his life out.

Years later Johnny admitted: 'In the wild, nervous frenzy that the amphetamines produced, I could never catch up with the things that my mind could think of to do. I had to build things, and I'm not a carpenter. I had to fix things. I took my guitars apart and couldn't glue them back together right. I would stay up all night writing to people that I hardly knew.'

Eventually the drugs induced hallucinations and Johnny even began hearing voices – voices that he couldn't ignore and which wouldn't go away. Those voices told him to 'have another bennie' or 'drink another beer'. To Cash, a God-fearing man, these terrifying incidents were made worse when that voice told him, 'Nothing can kill you.' Johnny later recalled: 'After long periods of being up and high for days, I'd finally give up and give into rest. Then the raging voices quietened and the evil presences left me, there would move in about me a gentle, warm, sweet presence and still, a small voice would breathe forth inside my being. "I am your

God. I am still here. I am still waiting. I still love you." And I would sleep.'

One of Johnny's best friends at the time was singer Merle Kilgore. They'd first met at fellow country artist Johnny Horton's home just before Johnny was killed in that auto accident back in 1960. Johnny had started taking pills around the same time. One night Kilgore tried to hypnotise Johnny to stop him taking the pills. But that effort failed miserably and Johnny simply swallowed back even more tablets.

Eventually, Merle became so fed up with his friend that he started avoiding Johnny purposely because he'd become so morose and such unpleasant company. Johnny eventually became ashamed to face Merle and they lost touch with each other for years. Johnny acknowledged it was a friendship he never truly appreciated, although they did eventually reconnect.

Although it's true that Johnny got to know Elvis Presley quite well back in Memphis, the two singing stars lost touch once Johnny moved to California. A few years later, Elvis showed up in Hollywood to do a movie entitled *G.I. Blues* and rented the top floor of the Beverly Wilshire Hotel for himself and his notorious entourage of hangers-on. Johnny paid Elvis a visit early one evening and was appalled by what he witnessed, despite his own serious problems with pills. He later described 'the bunch of moochers that hung after him' and found himself appalled at how much Elvis was paying out just to feed this virtual mini-army of so-called 'friends and associates'.

It seemed to Johnny that Elvis was enclosing himself in a little world. Johnny knew he had no place in Elvis's bizarre world and decided not to make any effort to see him ever again. Johnny walked out of the hotel that evening, saddened by the end of his friendship with Elvis. He still needed a daily supply of pills to keep his strength up but it made him think about all the time and effort he was wasting.

For the moment, however, the drugs continued to take centre stage. Months later in Las Vegas, Johnny was so wrecked by pills and booze that the legendary singer Roger Miller had to take over his show for him. Miller called himself an expert on 'pillology' and called Johnny 'Running Dilating Cash'. It was a cold, but fair reflection of Johnny's physical state at this time. Miller ended up taking Johnny's place every night for the following week.

Throughout all this, Johnny Cash somehow managed to retain his place as a regular on *The Grand Ole Opry*, even though he often missed show dates because of 'laryngitis'. At one stage, he cancelled nine out of ten recording sessions especially booked by his producer.

One Saturday night in Nashville, Johnny arrived at the Ryman Auditorium to perform on *The Grand Ole Opry* having taken a nonstop diet of pills for weeks. His voice was shot to pieces and he was a bag of bones, his weight down to a mere 165 pounds. Johnny caught one glance of himself in the glass door at the theatre as he walked into the auditorium and shuddered. He couldn't ignore the damage he was inflicting on himself.

Up on stage that night, the band kicked off a song and Johnny tried to take the microphone off the stand but, in his nervous, druggy frenzy, he couldn't get it off. He grabbed and twisted it, but it wouldn't move. Then his frustration exploded in a fit of anger in front of the entire audience. There was a stunned silence from the crowd. This was Johnny Cash at his lowest point.

Finally, Johnny grabbed the mike stand, threw it down on the ground, then dragged it along the edge of the stage, smashing 52 footlights in the process. The broken glass shattered all over the stage and into the audience as Johnny walked through the glass splinters. The song ended abruptly and Johnny stumbled offstage to come face to face with the manager of The Grand Ole Opry, who quietly and considerately informed Cash, 'We can't use you on the Opry any more, John.' Cash couldn't reply. He'd straightened himself out the moment the manager approached and knew he had no one else to blame but himself.

Johnny walked out of the back door of The Grand Ole Opry House, got in his car and drove off. After a few blocks, he headed south through the residential areas of Nashville to avoid police cars on the main highways. Tears were rolling down his cheeks as the reality of what had just happened began to dawn on him; he could hardly see through the windshield because of them. Then it began to rain and, as Johnny reached to turn on the windshield wipers, the car swerved and crashed into a tree on the sidewalk.

Johnny woke up a few hours later in a hospital emergency room with a broken nose and a broken jaw. The car was a write-off. Through the pain and anguish, Johnny felt desperately lonely and afraid. But, even now, he still couldn't imagine a life without drugs ...

10

LOSING THE WAY

One night in Chicago, Johnny Cash surpassed even his own lowly standards. He'd just finished a singing engagement at 10:30pm and decided that since the night was still young he'd hit a particular club in the city's blues district, where his new friend Charley Pride was playing. He returned to his hotel, grabbed a night's supply of pills to pop, plus a briefcase full of beers, and headed out to find Charley.

But, by the time Johnny hailed a cab outside his hotel, he was so far gone he couldn't even remember the name of the club. The cabbie thought it was his lucky night when Johnny brazenly announced he wanted to be taken to every club in town until he found the right place.

When the driver lit a marijuana joint and offered it to Johnny, he initially refused it.

'Aw, come on, man. You're on something. A little grass ain't gonna hurt.'

'How d'you know I'm on somethin'?' asked Johnny, feeling uncomfortable because it was plainly so obvious.

'Takes one to know one,' smiled the cabbie and passed Johnny the joint.

This time Cash took it and sucked in a mouthful of pungent smoke. Soon he was completely stoned as he and the driver began a crazy club-hopping night, fuelled by pot, beer and pills. They never did find Charley Pride in those clubs, and Cash later recalled he was lucky to get back to the hotel alive when – at 6:00am next morning – he walked into his room, grabbed a glass of water and chased it with a handful of tranquillisers. The 'downers' were supposed to counter the uppers he'd greedily consumed earlier. Johnny lay down on the bed and drifted into unconsciousness. He later admitted he hoped they'd wipe away the guilt he felt about what he'd just done. His tortured soul continued to haunt him.

There were many other similar incidents. Like the time, for example, Johnny 'escaped' in his luxury camper to the Mojave Desert, in California, with father Ray and good pal Curly Lewis, who owned the construction company that had built Johnny's house in Encino, near Los Angeles. But what Ray and Curly didn't realise was that Johnny had swallowed back yet another handful of pills before setting off on the journey and his head was soon spinning. Spotting a gate off the main highway that read: 'No trespassing. US Naval Proving Grounds – USN Ordinance', Johnny swerved the van across the road and drove at full speed right through the gate muttering, 'What's the Navy doing out here?' That gate was soon flapping in the wind.

Three miles of dirt track later they found themselves in the middle of a cratered runway that was being used for bombing practice. When the military police appeared in Johnny's rear-view mirror he took them on a five-minute chase. Yet, somehow, he escaped with nothing more than a ticking off.

Ray Cash was so upset he decided there and then never to take any more trips with his son up to the mountains. He was deeply concerned about Johnny's condition and convinced that he'd end up dead very soon if he didn't stop popping pills. Johnny was too high most of the time to even acknowledge the concern of those around him, though.

At home, wife Vivian watched on in horror, powerless to act as Johnny continued his one-way path to self-destruction. Many of those around him didn't quite realise the full extent of his involvement with drugs. Besides wrecking every car he'd owned for seven years, he wrote off two jeeps and a camper van as well as turning over two tractors and a bulldozer. He also sank two boats in separate accidents on a lake. Then there was the time he jumped from a truck just before it went over a six-hundred-foot cliff in California.

Despite Cash's rare visits home, Vivian became pregnant for a fourth time and, on August 24, 1961, she gave birth to yet another daughter, Tara. By this stage it was difficult to tell if Johnny had even noticed the new baby. He popped back to see mother and child but was back on the road within hours.

Whenever Johnny managed to avoid the pills, he became the perfect father and husband. At home in Casitas Springs, he installed a ten-foot aluminium cross, which he lit up for Christmas and Easter. Local churches sometimes borrowed it for Easter sunrise services. At Christmas, Johnny even hauled a hundred-pound amplifier on to the roof of his mansion and serenaded the entire valley with carols. Some neighbours begged Johnny to keep doing it every year, while others complained bitterly. In the end, the local sheriff had to ask him to turn the music off.

'People felt he was colourful, crazy Johnny,' recalled Joe Paul Jr, managing editor of Johnny's local rag, the *Ventura Star-Free Press*. 'They accepted it, pretty much. Why shouldn't he be colourful, they felt.'

Johnny formed an especially close friendship with leathery, Bible-quoting preacher the Reverend Floyd Gressett, who was delighted when the singer started attending his church in Ventura. Cash became an official member of the congregation six months later and he'd often sing at the church, the non-denominational Avenue Community Church.

Johnny nicknamed his pastor friend 'Chief' and gave him some walkie-talkies and a hunting knife as a gift. Gressett nicknamed Johnny 'Slick' and gave him a spare key to his ranch ninety miles north of Ventura, insisting he use it whenever he needed peace and solitude. Unfortunately, Johnny took full advantage of the churchman's offer and ended up popping pills at the ranch for days at a time.

Gressett encouraged Johnny to be more generous with his time. When local groups, such as the Ventura Boys Club, solicited help in fundraising, Cash agreed to give them a hand. The churchman had succeeded in teaching Johnny to give as well as take.

While Johnny was happy to help out worthwhile causes, he didn't seem capable of helping himself and his disregard for his own personal safety continued apace. In California, he bought a camper truck and painted the windows black so that he could sleep inside. He also used it for hunting and fishing as well as touring. One time, he was driving down Coldwater Canyon, near Los Angeles with a tank of propane gas for his camper sitting in the boot of his convertible. It leaked out and sparked a huge explosion as Johnny sat in a heavy traffic jam. The fire rapidly engulfed the drop-top vehicle. Before paramedics could get to the scene, Johnny was caught by the flames and received first-degree burns to the face and left wrist. The $8,000 car was destroyed. Not long afterwards he wrote off his camper following a horrific, drug-induced solo drive into the Californian desert. Crazed with narcotics, he looked in the rear-view mirror, stopped the vehicle and then, he later recalled, put his hand over his face, peeped through his fingers and said to himself, 'Let's kill us.'

He then screamed back at himself, 'I can't be killed. I'm indestructible.'

Looking himself in the eyes, he added, 'Dare you to try.'

Cash later openly admitted that he started the engine of the camper up again and started driving down a mountain. The camper lost control and flipped over twice, but Johnny only sustained a broken jaw. The battle within him was raging at full strength – fuelled by pills and booze – but would he survive it?

Some time later, Cash was clearing brush from the hillside of his Casitas Springs home with a tractor, when he bulldozed up a nest of rattlesnakes. Johnny – who had a phobia about snakes – jumped clear of the tractor as it rolled to a stop. But then an engine spark ignited the dry grass and Johnny was forced to hot-foot it to the house for help as the flames looked set to engulf the house. The front door was locked, though, and Vivian was inside listening to Elvis Presley records, so she didn't hear him. Eventually he raised the alarm by smashing a bedroom window, cutting his forearm in the process, and grabbing the nearest phone.

When the fire brigade arrived, Johnny evacuated his wife and four daughters in his limousine, but the bumper caught a firehose and yanked it off one of the trucks. The jolt threw the car out of control, breaking the steering-tie rod, though luckily no one was hurt and the fire was put out before it reached the house.

Cash also continued to believe he was hearing voices in his head, although it was obvious to others that these demons were actually just symptomatic of Johnny's paranoia coming through his pill-induced haze. His pill popping had left him guilt-ridden and he felt even worse when he was stoned while singing religious songs. He was ashamed to be in such a state whilst praying to God.

Although he didn't realise it at the time, one of Cash's best moves was to form a troupe of musical performers designed to tour under the banner 'The Johnny Cash Show'. They included the popular Statler Brothers and the immensely respected Carter Family. Johnny had never forgotten his earlier encounters with matriarch Maybelle Carter and her daughters, and had soon realised they were good people to have around. They were kind-spirited people, always offering him something to eat, or a glass of milk; one of them even happily ironed Johnny's shirt before he went on stage. Johnny had been a fan of The Carter Family since he was a kid; Maybelle and her sisters had been recording music since 1927. Johnny had never forgotten hearing June Carter on *The Grand Ole Opry* in 1950, when he was still living in Arkansas.

Johnny was in awe of Maybelle, whom he saw as an immensely strong-willed, tough-talking lady. He knew only too well that she'd made it in the world of country music without taking so much as a glass of alcohol, let alone a bucketful of pills. Maybelle was actually much more gentle than her public image and even later admitted, 'I don't know why he was scared of me, I wasn't gonna hurt the boy.'

Johnny's fear of Maybelle was really a form of utter respect, because she'd been one of the major influences on the country music scene at that time. Later, in 1966, she was even officially certified the Mother of Country Music in an emotional ceremony on the stage of The Grand Ole Opry. Eventually, she also made it to the Country Music Hall of Fame.

The Carters soon became a security blanket for Johnny during all those difficult years of drug-taking. Maybelle's beautiful young daughter June seemed particularly protective towards Johnny. June had been performing since the age of ten and delighted audiences with her tomboyish style and sense of humour. As a child back in what can only be described as 'Poor Valley', she'd played with her cousins in the woods where they'd take little pieces of brush and make little houses out of them to crawl into. But June later concluded that she really preferred being on her own a lot of the time. In many ways it was all very similar to Johnny Cash's upbringing.

Dancing was considered 'sinful' where the Carters grew up in Mace's Spring, Virginia, and their social life revolved around the prayer meetings and revivals at the Mount Vernon Methodist Church up on the hill behind their home. Often, little June Carter sneaked off into the hills and danced alone with a piece of chiffon in the high meadows. June was a tomboy: she was able to drive a relative's lumber truck from the age of fourteen; she was fond of wearing filthy overalls and was not all that bothered about taking baths too frequently. She also played a mean solid guitar and a five-string banjo, as well as being able to sing. Still in her teens, June married a country singer named Carl Smith, but the marriage crumbled after just a few months. That's when June 'escaped' to the bright lights of New York, where she tried her hand at acting by enrolling at the Neighborhood Playhouse – which later helped develop the careers of stars such as Tom Cruise. At one stage, June even tried her hand at stand-up comedy ('Sit down, squat down or lie down, but, honey, make yourself at home!' was her favourite introductory one-liner to audiences).

June's long-flowing hair and friendly demeanour had men lining up at her door in New York, so it was no surprise to her family when she married once again – to an ex-football player named Rip Nixon. Soon she added motherhood to her long list of youthful achievements.

Despite having a family, June adored touring with Johnny Cash and admitted that she felt extremely maternal towards him from the moment they linked up on the road. June immediately recognised Cash's drug-taking as a cry for help from a man at war with himself. She believed Johnny to be a warm, caring man whose constant battles with those inner demons were threatening to destroy his life. She heard all about the bomb pranks and his highly strung side. She felt she soon knew exactly who she was dealing with and she certainly wasn't in awe of the big man.

Only a week after June officially joined The Johnny Cash Show, the singer asked her to sew up a pair of his ripped pants when the troupe were staying overnight at a motel. June set to with a needle and thread and, since it was a warm day, left the room door open. Within minutes, 'gang' members – including Cash, Marshall and Perkins – were walking past her room on their way to the restaurant when they came upon a large pickling barrel crammed with confetti.

'What June needs is an official welcome,' whispered Marshall to the others. The trio then appeared at June's door with the barrel, and told her how happy they were to have her along and then emptied the confetti, knee-deep, all over the room.

'Lord, what are you *doing*?' asked June, by now standing on her bed.

'Don't worry, June,' reassured Johnny. 'We'll clean it up. We want to show you how good we are at cleanin' things up.'

Band member Fluke Holland and Marshall then lugged in a massive rubber-tyred lawn cleaner that they had commandeered from the hotel poolman. They cranked it up and, with a roar from the cleaner as the big canvas bag popped out of the right side, they began sweeping the room. It started sucking up the confetti but then ran out of gas.

Then they wrestled the huge machine out of the room, making their apologies about it breaking down. June pushed aside Johnny's trousers and spent the rest of the day cleaning up the room with a borrowed broom and dustpan. She never complained to them and they decided she must have figured it had been the initiation ceremony.

June's obsessive tidiness quickly became the running joke of the troupe. One time, Cash and his pals started breaking empty soda bottles in a dressing room just before a show. June asked them to stop after saying the noise frightened her. But that simply encouraged them to throw even more bottles. June then lost her temper, knocked over a coatrack full of hangers, grabbed up her own armful of soda bottles and threw every single one at Johnny and his trio. In the end they begged her to quit. 'And I never had any more trouble with them after that,' she later recalled.

June deliberately avoided confronting Johnny about his drug addiction at first. For more than six months she sat back and observed him, sometimes shocked by his condition, but unable to bring herself to interfere. The first big clue was the vast quantity of water Johnny was consuming; then she noticed that he frequently excused himself to find a doctor, and after one show she caught him with a handful of pills. She'd seen it all before with the legendary Hank Williams. June later recalled: 'It was none of my business. But, when you work with someone, you get close. It's like a family. I felt responsible for him in some ways.'

Even through his drug-induced haze, Johnny knew June had a soft spot for him, but he was in no fit state to return her attention, so he just let it pass. In any case, he didn't really give a damn who knew what he was doing at this stage in his career. Johnny was treated with such awe and hero worship that no one had the courage to tell him a few home truths.

The early sultry looks that won Johnny Cash a following across the world.

The King of Country with the King of Rock 'n' Roll – Cash and Elvis in a rare picture together.

A rare publicity poster for *Johnny Cash: The Man, His World, His Music.*

Top: Johnny Cash and his band playing the historic concert at Folsom Prison.

Bottom: Johnny with Kirk Douglas in a still from *A Gunfight*.

Johnny's appearance on Bob Dylan's *Nashville Skyline* album brought his talents to a whole new audience. The two seminal artists are pictured here together.

Johnny with his wife, performer June Carter Cash, and their newborn baby John.

The Johnny Cash show attracted all the most important artists of the time.
Here Ray Charles and Johnny perform together.

A face that tells of a lifetime of hard living. Johnny Cash: 1932-2003.

On May 10, 1962, Johnny joined other country stars for a show at Carnegie Hall with his drug- and smoke-ravaged voice in a terrible state. Johnny – dressed up in a railroader's cap and jacket and carrying a lighted lantern as a tribute to the first legend of country music, Jimmie Rodgers – gave such an inaudible performance that producer Don Law didn't bother to switch on recording equipment for a planned live album of the star's songs.

His drug addiction was not helped by the ridiculous schedule he kept agreeing to. In November, 1962, he volunteered to visit US troops stationed in Korea and in the course of one week sang to 26,000 GIs, roughly half the entire number stationed in Korea. He was scheduled to do twenty shows but ended up doing thirty and once home had to be hospitalised with acute laryngitis. For some weeks afterwards, he completely lost his voice.

At home, Johnny and his kid brother Tommy had a serious fallout. The younger Cash worked for the singer, handling all his fan mail and correspondence. Then, completely out of the blue, Tommy was approached by a recording company and offered a four-song contract. Tommy juggled the deal and his job for Johnny and began sending out his own record and fan pictures with Johnny Cash promotional mailings. He also wrote a song called 'I Didn't Walk The Line', which blatantly cashed in on the title of his brother's hit record. The record bombed badly and Tommy quit his brother's office after a series of clashes. It took some time for them to mend the fence that grew between them.

Another problem on the drug front was that some of Johnny's best friends were also on pills. Cash remained incredibly loyal to them, especially the ones whose lives had been wrecked by drugs. One time, Johnny bought his pal a record player and a stack of discs, which he took in when visiting Travis in a North Hollywood drying-out clinic. It was Cash's way of saying get well soon.

Johnny also became involved in the highly emotive subject of the plight of Native Americans by putting out an album, *Bitter Tears*, featuring songs that told of their struggle for real recognition. 'The Ballard of Ira Hayes' told the true story of the Native American who, as a marine, helped raise the American flag at Iwo Jima, but returned home to die as a civilian drunk in a ditch. The country music world seemed to shy away from Johnny's controversial opinions; for his part, Cash himself became convinced he was one-quarter Cherokee.

Johnny Cash was so irritated by the music business snub to *Bitter Tears* that he paid thousands of dollars to put an advertisement in *Billboard* magazine accusing other musicians and technicians in the industry of being afraid of the truth. The editor of one country music magazine called on Cash to resign from the Country Music Association: 'You and your crowd are just too intelligent to associate with plain country folks, country artists and country DJs,' said the commentator. People started to accuse Johnny Cash of thinking himself too big for the country music scene.

At around this time, Johnny also made a rare solo appearance without his Tennessee Three when he guested on the folk music TV series *Hootenanny*, which featured Maybelle Carter. Being alongside Maybelle made Johnny feel the Carters really did represent his 'other' family. Maybelle had fathomed out Johnny better than anyone else, including his own mother and father.

Meanwhile, Johnny was carrying around so many pills that, whenever he looked for change in his pockets, tablets would spill all over the floor. Thankfully, he never graduated to being a 'speed freak' mainlining amphetamines with a hypodermic, as many other addicts did, but sometimes, when the pills took hold, they unleashed a mindless violence he could scarcely control.

Eventually June, encouraged by her mother, took it upon herself to sort Cash out. One day – playing at the Mint, in Las Vegas – she spotted Johnny dropping a handful of white pills from his pocket as he was about to go on stage. June glared at him for a split second and Johnny caught her glance before looking down sheepishly. Then, as she put it later, 'I lit into him like a circular saw.' Cash, in his drugged-up deluded state, didn't welcome the interference and totally ignored June's outrage.

A couple of times, he later admitted, he came close to hurting her physically – like the night she threw away his pills and he screamed at her, 'If you weren't a woman, I'd break your neck.'

June didn't flinch. She just answered back calmly, 'You'd miss me.' And Johnny knew she was absolutely right.

Anyway, June wouldn't give up that easily. She'd sensed that her interest in Johnny Cash had become more than just maternal. Despite the drugs, the booze and the aggressive behaviour, something was drawing her closer and closer to him. She was falling in love with him. Her marriage to Rip Nixon was drifting apart but it left her feeling terrible about yet another failed marriage and being in love with a married man was consuming her with guilt. June tried to hold back for as long as she could and in the meantime steeled herself to continue her one-woman campaign to get Johnny off the booze and the pills.

Some nights on tour, when Johnny was away from his hotel suite, June and Carl Perkins would search his room. They always found hundreds of pills in various hiding places and immediately flushed them down the toilet. June would then confront Johnny, telling him, 'You're a better man than that, and you're not goin' on stage that way. I have an excuse if I give a bad performance, because I don't have as much talent as you do.' After such blatant confrontations, Johnny would usually throw away the pills and continue the tour smoothly, but once back home, he'd always restock his run-down supplies.

Johnny continued feeling guilty about what he was doing. He knew it was wrong, but he just didn't have the strength to fight his addiction. Beneath the surface, he adored June for what she was trying to do, but he was too far gone to show his true emotions. The reality was that Johnny Cash – the Arkansas boy made good – had not let his feet touch the ground in years. He'd virtually lost touch with reality. Everyone around him was telling him how marvellous he was, how talented – and he was certainly rich. He felt invincible and the nonstop drugs simply fuelled that illusion.

• • • •

For the young all over the free world to whom President John F Kennedy seemed like half-messiah and half-movie star, his death in November, 1963 ushered in a decade of violence, sociopolitical upheaval and cultural change. Vietnam, the antiwar movement, campus unrest, the assassinations of Robert Kennedy and Martin Luther King, riots, the violence at the 1968 Democratic Convention in Chicago, the Black Panthers, LBJ and Richard Nixon, hippies, yippies, free sex, Woodstock, Altamont, acid heads and acid rock, the Manson Family – these are some of the features that defined the turbulent 1960s and early 1970s. Few people were to be *less* identified with this age of discontent and institution-smashing than Johnny Cash.

In the months following John Kennedy's assassination, it became increasingly evident that America could not return to the relative tranquillity of the early postwar years. In 1964, the Warren Commission Report concluded that Lee Harvey Oswald had acted alone in killing the President, and a jury in turn convicted Dallas nightclub owner Jack Ruby of murdering Oswald. That was also the year three civil-rights workers – Goodman, Cheney and Schwerner – were murdered in Philadelphia, Mississippi, to the outrage of a nation.

In August, 1964, North Vietnamese torpedo boats allegedly attacked the US destroyers *Maddox* and *Turner Joy*. President Lyndon Johnson, seizing the opportunity to escalate the war effort in South-East Asia, ordered retaliatory air strikes. The Tonkin Gulf Resolution, passed overwhelmingly by Congress five days later, gave the President authority to take any steps he deemed necessary to 'maintain peace'.

So it was, amongst the peace worshippers and antiwar brigade, that the unlikely figure of Johnny Cash emerged a hero at the Newport Folk Festival, in 1964. He even gave his new friend Bob Dylan his Martin guitar as a gesture of respect and solidarity that must have confused all those who wondered what Johnny was doing with the long-haired weirdo – to say nothing of those who wondered what Dylan was doing hanging around with those Southern bigot shit-kickers down in Nashville.

Johnny Cash forged a surprisingly close relationship with Bob Dylan when they both appeared at Newport. Johnny even went to the trouble of writing to folk song magazine *Broadside* to defend Dylan's decision to play an electric guitar at the festival the following year, which horrified so-called purists of the folk scene.

By 1965 Johnny Cash had all but hit rock bottom in personal terms. Professionally, he was setting all-time records for touring, having scored spectacular success with a number-one hit, 'Ring of Fire' in 1963. But, despite this success, Cash now had a reputation in the industry as 'the worst no-show in the business'. Numerous venues across the country were filing law suits against him, many of which would take years to go through the court system.

That same year, Cash was arrested by narcotics agents in El Paso, Texas. It was the culmination of a specially supervised operation to trap the pill-popping singer who'd been down to Juarez, in Mexico, where a black market for such pills thrived. Cash was picked up as he crossed back into the United States and was boarding a plane in Texas. When detained just minutes before take-off, the singer had 688 Dexedrine and 475 Equanil tablets tucked into his pockets and hidden inside his precious guitar, along with

$12,000 in cash. He was immediately thrown into El Paso Jail – which proved, by all accounts, to be a sobering experience for him. His cell hadn't been cleaned since the previous occupant. The plumbing didn't work. There wasn't even a mattress or a pillow – just a dirty blanket over the bed springs. The lights stayed on all night. And as Johnny lay there watching roaches crawl across the floor he heard some of the other inmates laughing and cursing at each other.

Halfway through the night, Johnny heard a boy crying – either in fear at his predicament or because he was being raped by another prisoner. Johnny listened to another man praying which, he later explained, inspired him to try to pray, but he couldn't. Instead, he began crying, thinking about his family and his friends and how he'd let them all down.

The next day, a bond was posted and Johnny got out. But then he had to face an army of press photographers and soon snaps of Johnny being led away in handcuffs were being wired around the world. The singer's secret addiction was now out in the open for the first time. Johnny later recalled that day as being the lowest point of his career. The shame of it forced him to sober up, and the shock of his arrest definitely had a positive short-term effect on his drug intake. Laying off the pills had some obvious and immediate benefits: Cash gained twenty pounds very rapidly and started to lose that pallid complexion, the haunted look that people had become so used to they just presumed it was the way he was meant to be. The change in his appearance was so drastic that at his next concert the promoter ordered softer, blue spotlights to be used on the stage because 'he looked like a truck had hit him'. For that six-week period Cash was off the pills, he started to get into pretty good shape. But then one night he felt the stress bearing down on him once more and began drifting back to his old, nasty habits. Soon the pills had returned with a vengeance.

In December, 1965, Johnny had to make a court appearance in connection with that earlier arrest in El Paso. Wire services across the country snapped a photo of the singer, accompanied by wife Vivian, walking down the El Paso Courthouse steps following his arraignment. A shadow darkened Vivian's face in the photo and soon the picture was running in *Thunderbolt*, a racist magazine published by the Ku Klux Klan. An article beneath the picture concluded that Johnny was 'scum' and had married a 'negress' who bore him 'mongrelized children'. Soon KKK fanatics and fellow right-wing racists were flooding Johnny's organisation with death threats against the star.

Weakened though he was by pills, Johnny was understandably infuriated by the attacks. His boyhood in Dyess, Arkansas, had given him very little contact with black people and he felt no particular emotional bias. But he recognised that the accusation was a calculated attempt to undercut his popularity where it was strongest, amongst white Southerners. He was outraged.

Then the Klan sent word that Cash would be assassinated if he dared to play an upcoming date in South Carolina. Although strung out on pills and exhausted from his already gruelling schedule, Johnny played the date anyway and defied the death threats heroically. No one was going to intimidate him. Even the drugs couldn't water down that determination.

Unfortunately, Johnny had underestimated the power of the Klan and the degree to which it could inflame passions. The rumour of his so-called 'mongrelized children' continued to spread like a roaring forest fire throughout the South. In some places, bookings were cancelled. In others, sales of Cash records dramatically fell off. His problem was how to fight the Klan and discredit it without at the same time giving the impression that he felt there was something wrong in being married to a black woman.

Finally, Johnny decided the only way to win his battle against the bigots was to publicly deny the facts in the Klan's pamphlet. That way, perhaps, if people understood the Klan had been wrong in this instance they might realise the Klan could be wrong about everything else. He announced he was suing the KKK for $25 million. The threats continued. When Johnny turned up to record a new track with Don Law, a reporter tipped him off that a Klan 'wrecking party' was cruising around Nashville threatening to 'get Cash'. While Johnny was in the recording session, a green sedan pulled up outside and asked the black doorman if Johnny was there. The man claimed he didn't know, but then rushed inside to inform Johnny and Don of what had happened. Johnny had been expecting trouble and was toting a shotgun borrowed from June Carter's father. He rushed outside to confront his enemies, but they'd gone.

That night Johnny slept in Don Law's small Nashville apartment. Law had a canister of tear gas at hand for protection and Johnny still had that shotgun by his side. Unfortunately, as Law was shaving next morning, a friend dropped by the apartment, picked up the canister and began fiddling with it. The canister exploded and tear gas swirled through the apartment, much to everyone's embarrassment.

Not surprisingly, the smear campaign against Cash soon ran out of steam; most people recognised it as outrageous falsity. A tiny minority of so-called fans, suckered in by the Klan's claims, did attempt to spit in his face in public places. Johnny held his temper and instead pressed ahead with his legal action against the Klan. Eventually, he had to allow the legal action drop, but he let it be known everywhere that he'd never forgive or forget the Klan.

At around this time, producer Don Law managed to squeeze another album out of Johnny thanks to his good patience and understanding of the star's continuing drug addiction problems. Law knew that Johnny's voice was shaky at best and sometimes he couldn't sing a lick, but he still believed in him.

In the middle of all this, Johnny Cash was still riding high in terms of record sales despite the onset of the British pop groups who had dominated the music industry since The Beatles first arrived in the States a year earlier. Many of the stars of Johnny's early days had already fallen by the wayside for a variety of reasons. Roy Orbison was suffering badly. He'd had seventeen hits before 1965 and only five thereafter. In the same period The Platters dropped from twenty hits to two, Johnny Mathis from eighteen to two, The Drifters from sixteen to none, Connie Francis from thirty-five to none and Brenda Lee from twenty-seven to two. But Johnny did not suffer any fall-off, which was quite an achievement in itself. On the other hand, his personal fortune was ebbing away, through a combination of overgenerosity to his family and friends, and phenomenal squandering, thanks in part to those excessive drug habits.

Cash eventually produced an album with June Carter entitled *Carrying On*. It was one of his best to date, though by now his weight had dropped from 200 pounds to nearly 140 and he looked deeply unhealthy on the album sleeve. Producer Don Law later recalled how he'd start a recording session at six in the evening and end up next morning with nothing. A young songwriter called Kris Kristofferson came to Nashville in April 1966, 'dragging down a cool fifty-eight bucks a week', in his own words, as a studio man for Columbia. Kristofferson sneaked into Cash's recording sessions but later recalled: 'It was painful. John would come in and many hours would go by and nothing would happen. He was wasted, but electric to watch.'

During one session, Cash ripped up a handful of suggested album covers, lit several cigarettes at the same time, tore his shirt open and then began recording 'John Henry', a dramatic eight-minute narrative that he'd revised from the original folk ballad. Cash accompanied himself with two bars of cold-rolled steel that he banged together. When he'd finished, his hands were bloody. He'd battered them between the bars without feeling any pain.

Kristofferson soon found there was only one way to Johnny Cash's heart. Kristofferson had made it as a Rhodes Scholar at Oxford and then as a helicopter pilot, but kept losing out in Nashville. His long-suffering and exhausted wife had just given up on him and departed for California with their two kids. Then he was booted out of a Cash recording session because a few friends had sneaked in to pitch some songs. The following night, Kristofferson was working down in the boiler room at the studio when Johnny Cash walked in, borrowed a smoke and invited him up to the new session. Kristofferson hesitated and explained that he'd been barred. 'Well,' said Cash, 'I ain't singin' without you, kid.' When the two walked into the studio together, the session finally got under way. Cash was soon plugging the broke young man as a songwriter, which Kristofferson recognised as a 'helluva endorsement'.

Cash had an uncanny ability to recognise in others his own weaknesses. It was just a shame he couldn't see his own faults so clearly.

11

'I'LL HAVE TO TREAT YOU AS
IF YOU'RE A CHILD'

Johnny Cash and his troupe were often seen at their best at
the summer fairs that turn up in cities across the South
Central states of America. Hours before his performances,
stadiums would be packed to bursting point. Umbrellas
sprouting against the sun. Working men in sports shirts,
collegians in cut-off Levi's, waitresses in beehive hairdos and
tight slacks, and motherly looking types in print dresses
waiting patiently as the sun lowered and a faint breeze
brought the special aroma of country fairs, a pungent
essence of dust, hamburgers, animal sweat, beer, manure,
watermelon rinds and alfalfa. Men in the audiences would
struggle through the crowds to the midway for foot-long
hotdogs with chilli and giant orangeades. A handful of town
police would wander gently amongst the crowds.

Just minutes before the show was to begin, Cash would

send out his three groups – The Carter Family, The Tennessee Three and The Statler Brothers. Then Johnny himself would stride on to the platform. The crowd would rise to its feet. Husband and wives, many middle-aged, would raise their arms in rapture. That's when he'd give his classic introduction, 'Hello. I'm Johnny Cash,' and break into a song. His short patent leather boots, with red heels and soles, twisted in a little dance as his big frame wheeled around. Then he'd pull his favourite Martin guitar high up on his chest, crimp his right arm lightly over the top of it and run his fingers far out on the neck of the instrument and back to the other end.

Creaks of perspiration would soon lace his cheeks. It was hard work. 'Gene Autry once said,' recalled Johnny years later, 'if it weren't so hard, everybody would be doin' it.' Before another number, he'd lower his guitar and tell a story, his eyes looking out above the faces to the south-west, towards Arkansas, his birthplace. This was the Johnny Cash millions wanted and adored. Many of Johnny Cash's most fervent fans were in awe of their hero. 'He just melts you down,' said one. And the stage was undoubtedly the place where he felt most at home.

The *other* Johnny Cash landed in jail yet again in 1966 when he was arrested in Starkville, Mississippi – for picking flowers. As was becoming traditional for the Man in Black, he'd ignored posted signs and felt the urge to test authority. The sheriff who arrested him was not impressed by the celebrity status of his prisoner. Johnny later immortalised his experiences in a song called 'Starkville City Jail', which he included on his phenomenally successful *Johnny Cash at San*

Quentin album. Cash revealed his real attitude by telling audiences, 'You know, they told me, "You have to stand here, you have to sing these songs ..." and I told them, "Why don't you just let me do what the fuck I want to do?"'

Later in 1966, Johnny had some fun gunning his Cadillac down Highway 33 in California at 90 miles an hour, with a police cruiser in frantic pursuit. Once the cops pulled him over, Johnny told them, 'I wanted to see if I could still outrun a police car.' That little escapade cost him $56 at Ventura Municipal Court.

In June, 1966, Cash's roller-coaster lifestyle was further disturbed by the – hardly surprising – news that his wife Vivian was filing for divorce on the grounds of extreme cruelty. Although Johnny had known for some time that the marriage was in trouble, the news sent him spiralling further into druggy seclusion. He was locking his emotions up where no one in the world could reach them. And by now even June had all but given up her frantic efforts to get him to kick his pill habit.

Johnny Cash reacted to his impending divorce in the only way he knew how – by taking his life into an even more self-destructive mode. He frequently bedded down at producer Don Law's apartment in Nashville, which meant him coming in the front door, going through every drawer looking for drugs, trashing the rest of the place and then collapsing on the bed. Most times, Cash scrawled a note to his landlord along the following lines, 'Mr Law – I'm sleeping here – Hope you don't mind. I needed the rest. I'm ready to record that single. I need to talk to you later today, on an important business matter if you can, John.' Before he left, he usually fried up some bacon for breakfast. In the course of those visits, he managed to break the toaster and drop the coffee pot.

One rainy September night in 1966, Cash borrowed June Carter's Cadillac and careered off up the street until the inevitable occurred: he crashed the vehicle into a wall at 35 miles an hour and was knocked unconscious. Luckily for him, Gene Ferguson, Columbia Records' sales manager in Nashville, had just finished a meeting with Cash and was driving behind him. Cash had climbed out of the wreck and was staggering down the street when Ferguson overtook him outside an electrical repair shop and jumped out of his car. Holding Johnny, he turned the star's face up to the light. Blood was pouring from Johnny's nose and mouth on to his white shirt. Ferguson bundled him into the back seat of his car and drove him to the emergency room at the nearby Vanderbilt Hospital. Johnny woke up in hospital with yet another broken nose and four missing teeth, but he adamantly refused to stay overnight.

June and Carl Perkins took Johnny back to his home and put him to bed in the belief that he'd stay there the entire night. Next day, June Carter woke up to find Johnny collapsed in a coma in the living room. It later emerged that he'd stayed up all night and swallowed back a near-lethal combination of painkillers, amphetamines and booze. Johnny was rushed to hospital again, and this time he was lucky to pull through.

Friends and family were now convinced Johnny Cash wouldn't live much longer. The singer's downward slide could surely only end in one place. He'd lost a further forty pounds, his gaunt face now so skeletal that many didn't recognise him. Most of his friends had deserted him after coming to the conclusion that no amount of persuasion was going to get Johnny to admit his problem and actually change. Even Cash's days off were immersed in a haze of amphetamines and tranquillisers and, when he did go back on tour, he arrived for shows utterly exhausted.

Just before Christmas, 1966, Johnny – who'd been staying most of his time in Nashville between tours because of the crumbling state of his marriage – decided he had to see his daughters for the holidays, so on December 20 he left Tennessee with the express intention of flying straight to Los Angeles. But, when the plane stopped en route, he got off. He spent two sleepless nights in Dallas visiting just about every club in town, sitting with musicians, drinking with them and taking pills by the handful. Now and again he'd slip into some of the sleazier joints and watch those wicked women doing dances scantily clad and lots more besides. Next stop was Tucson, Arizona, and another whirlwind of clubs and bad company. He only finally made it to California on Christmas Eve and his homecoming wasn't really appreciated. The family had given up hope of him turning up in time for Christmas and he felt like a stranger in his own home.

Having filed for divorce, Vivian wanted only minimal contact with Johnny. His parents lived a few miles away near Ojai, so he took off for their house. They tried to bring up the subject of salvaging his marriage for the sake of the children, but Johnny wasn't capable of having a sensible conversation with them. Eventually, he went back to the family home and spent most of his time alone in the guest bedroom. In the background, he could hear his daughters opening their presents shrieking, 'Daddy is sick ... Daddy is tired.' As he lay there listening to the family he should have been with, it finally started to dawn on Cash that he'd caused the gulf between them. He'd missed out on so much of their childhood – the million little precious things that happened while 'Daddy was on the road'. Things like Tara losing her first tooth; the senior play; the children's birthdays; an Easter egg hunt. The list was endless.

Vivian was in no way responsible for the break-up of Johnny's marriage. She'd been a faithful wife, as good a mother as she knew how to be, and she'd made every effort to try and get Johnny to give up drugs. She'd find them and flush them down the toilet and she was always trying to get her husband to see a psychiatrist about his problems. But he'd been taking pills for years by then and it was too little too late.

It had never been easy for Vivian Liberto Cash. With four children separated by just seven years, she couldn't keep pace with her husband's sky-rocketing career. Cash's fame put intolerable pressure on their marriage. She hoped he'd stay the same man she'd married. But when the family moved out to California, the new home had spelled the beginning of the end.

The divorce became final on January 3, 1968, nearly a year and a half after Vivian had first filed suit. She was awarded a substantial property settlement and custody of the children. A mere eight days later, she married Richard Distin, a Ventura policeman who then left the force to take up hairdressing. Vivian's problems with Cash were partly based on her not being part of his set. She even insisted on calling him Johnny, even though he was 'John' to all his friends. Later, she was to become particularly upset by claims she'd driven him to take drugs because of her complete lack of interest in his career. But in Vivian's mind, she was never invited to be part of that side of his life. She had no choice. She later recalled: 'They all make it look like I got him on pills. But, if there was anything left to do, I did it. I tried everything in the book. Johnny knows to this day that I've never lied to him.'

Vivian never forgot one of the many times Johnny came home to their beautiful house in Casitas Springs, near LA, in a completely wrecked state. She'd pleaded with him, 'Please tell me what I can do to help you.'

Cash replied, 'I really appreciate it, but nobody can help me but myself.'

Vivian later looked back on her life in those last few years with Johnny Cash as being like a living hell. She never criticised him, because he was the father of her children. But it was impossible to entirely wipe away all those bad memories and she remained angry about all the things that her children had missed – a father who was there to encourage them, comfort them, advise, teach, direct, protect and love them.

On December 26, 1968, Johnny returned to Nashville a broken man. His family had fallen apart. His career was at a crisis point – he wasn't just missing the occasional concert now, whole tours were being cancelled because of his 'ill health'. Other acts were going ahead with the rest of the troupe after announcements that Johnny was sick were made to disappointed audiences over and over again.

By this time, Johnny was generally staying at the Carter family home in Nashville. June's father, Ezra, and her mother Maybelle would keep a room specially made up for whenever he wanted to drop by. They even gave Johnny a key to the house, which he promptly lost while out on a drug binge. One night Johnny called round at the house, found no one was in and simply kicked the door down to get in. That first time, Johnny fixed the door from the inside, but after a few such incidents the door became splintered beyond repair. He also managed to smash a number of windows by forcing them open.

Often Johnny would walk out of the Carter house in the middle of the night and start calling up all his old druggie friends. Then he'd drive into Nashville city centre where he'd end up being tossed out of a beer joint or hustled along some alley by a policeman on the beat. Cash was becoming known as the city's saddest joke. At other times, Johnny flopped overnight in local barns, stalked the woods and even sometimes appeared unexpectedly downtown on Music Row, ending up in strange rooms after calculated binges that left him more frenetic than ever.

Cash knew full well how badly he was abusing his friends' kindness. In an effort to start straightening himself out, he rented an apartment in nearby Madison, Tennessee. It was a modest one-bedroomed place with a kitchen and living room. The first night Johnny stayed there he felt incredibly lonely and – filled with his customary intake of pills – paced the floor until dawn muttering to himself, 'This ain't the answer, gettin' away by myself when I can't *stand* myself.'

Next day in downtown Nashville, Johnny ran into Waylon

Jennings, who'd just come into town. It was a perfect opportunity for Johnny to have some much-needed company and he persuaded Jennings to move into his apartment. Jennings was shocked by the messy way Johnny lived and immediately spring-cleaned the entire place. Unfortunately, a bond of friendship was never to form between the two stars because Jennings was out day and night in Nashville.

Jennings soon realised Cash was using vast quantities of pills. Johnny was so out of his head he actually thought his fellow country singer was on the same sort of uppers as himself. One night, when Jennings had gone to bed, Cash became so desperate for some drugs that he broke into his friend's car, which stood parked outside their apartment. Cash later recalled: 'I got a screwdriver and started prying open the door of the glove compartment. I rammed the screwdriver in the crack and pulled hard. The tough, brittle plastic door shattered into a million pieces, and I looked inside, pulling papers, letters, tapes, everything but pills, out on to the floor.' Waylon Jennings never confronted Johnny Cash about his broken glove compartment. But a few weeks later, when Jennings and Johnny were sitting in the living room of the apartment singing and writing, Jennings asked him why he lived in such a crummy little place when he had so much money.

'Guess I'd feel guilty about buying another house with my girls in California,' came the nervous reply from Cash.

'Get yourself a nice house and maybe their mother will let them visit you,' responded Jennings.

Cash got in his car that afternoon and drove east, out through Hendersonville, in Sumner County. He'd long admired the beautiful countryside past Hendersonville, where the hills rolled gracefully amongst the beef and dairy farms and tobacco patches, on to an idyllic spot called Old Hickory Lake. This was classic Andrew Jackson territory, the lake being named after 'Old Hickory' himself.

Johnny Cash turned off the highway and took a winding road down towards the lake near an area containing the homes of several entertainers and friends in showbusiness. There was Red Foley's house, Roy Acuff's and Lester Flatt's; on around the lake was Roy Orbison's home.

That's when Johnny Cash spotted a most unusual property down by the cove of the lake. He stopped his car, got out, walked down to the bank and looked at the 200-foot-long building that was still under construction. It contained two big, round 35-foot rooms, one on top of the other, on each end of the house. The centre part was all of 130 foot long and had a large kitchen and bathroom. The whole building was being built on a base of solid rock.

Just then the proud owner emerged. Johnny immediately asked him if he could buy the place, but the man insisted it was not for sale at any price. But Johnny Cash would not give up. He was convinced now that the house was meant to be his. As he later recalled: 'A few things have come along in my life that I knew were meant to be, and I know I was meant to live in that house.' A few days later, Johnny bought the house.

It seemed the perfect home to Johnny: rough timbers and stones, all on the wooded shores of Old Hickory Lake. It curved around the cliff of solid limestone into which it was set. Some of the house had a solid roof, with real grass growing out of it. It was big and roomy and rugged. The interior featured massive beams and stairways that circled upward to round, turretlike bedrooms. All over the house were hand-hewn logs salvaged from pioneer barns in the nearby Cumberland Mountains. On the grounds outside, a stream gurgling down out of a ravine was dammed up to form a swimming pool.

Johnny and the house's owner, Braxton Dixon, completed the transaction for that dream property over a can of beer. 'I'm not much into signing contracts,' said Cash. 'Neither am I,' agreed Braxton. So instead they just shook hands on it. Dixon was eventually to become a close friend.

Johnny moved in almost immediately, even though the place was only half finished. He considered it the perfect hide-out. Inside, he had one big bed and a mattress, but not a stick of furniture in sight.

The singer nailed up cardboard signs on the bushes of his new pride and joy: 'Trespassers are intruders. Intruders are law breakers and invaders. So you're pushing your luck if you don't belong here.' Cash stayed inside the house for days at a time, pacing the rough timber floors, trying to work out how to get a grip on his life. When his clothes got dirty he just threw them away and bought brand new ones.

At this time, Cash refused to open any mail except letters from his children, which he read again and again until they were dog-eared. Whenever Braxton found any of Johnny's stash of pills he'd throw them away without consulting the star. The house had a succession of telephones – when Johnny did not feel like answering the phone he would simply rip it out of the wall and throw it out of the window.

When Johnny did manage to come down from the pills and booze, he'd sleep it off over at Braxton's nearby house. Braxton's wife Anna would prepare Cash a big plate of home-made spaghetti or beans, which he'd scoop up with his hands. It seemed some habits died hard ...

May 20, 1967, was the 23rd anniversary of Johnny's brother Jack's death and it sparked off a vast pillfest for the tormented singer. Cash was still living in a bachelor-style apartment in one corner of the vast property. He announced to his family he wanted to hold a big dinner to commemorate the anniversary of his brother's death and persuaded his mother and father, brother Roy, sister Louise, sister Joann and brother Tommy to visit him in the new, uncompleted house.

Johnny's kid sister Reba called the family up for him. All of them thought Johnny was crazy, though they agreed to come all the same. Johnny even flew to California to travel back with his parents, who didn't want to fly alone. But on the plane, Johnny overdosed on barbiturates and had to be removed from the aircraft before it took off from Memphis to Nashville. Brother Tommy rounded on Johnny when he awoke from his drug-induced coma the following day.

'Don't you care what you're doin' to Mama and Daddy?' he screamed.

The star yelled back at his kid brother, who then took a swing at him. Johnny hit back and there was a scuffle. When it was over, Tommy looked at his brother with tears in his eyes, shook his head and walked away. When Johnny realised what he'd done he started sobbing.

The commemoration of Jack's death the next day was an

even bigger disaster. There was no table or chairs in the house, let alone beds for the guests. In the end, Johnny gave his parents his bed and he ended up on a sofa. The atmosphere was tense and Johnny's relatives couldn't wait to get out of that house. Johnny Cash seemed to have sunk about as low as a human being could get.

Plagued by troubles at home, Johnny Cash found it easier to cope with the problems of life back on the road. He'd wander off by himself, sometimes on foot, from the tour bus that carried the troupe. Marshall, who drove it, refused to give him the key. One time in Kingston, Ontario, Cash found a locksmith to grind out a new bus key and disappeared in the vehicle overnight. Another time, Johnny ground out the locks to June's mother Maybelle's white Cadillac and, whenever she drove it afterwards, her own key would keep falling out of the ignition. Johnny would disappear for hours, then reappear, often completely incoherent, minutes before a show, walk onstage and earn a screaming ovation.

The singer was prone to countless accidents, although he never seemed to damage himself seriously. His troupe members The Statler Brothers called it 'LOC' – the Luck of Cash. 'He's the luckiest person you could ever meet,' recalled Statler member Harold Reid. 'If he ever hit an old lady it would turn out she was wanted by the FBI.'

But the more he got away with things the more trouble he got into. Often at night, he'd patrol the hotel corridors slamming doors, washing the halls with a firehose; once, in Pennsylvania, he chopped his door apart with a fire axe out of sheer mental frustration. On that occasion, Marshall ran downstairs to soothe the management, but at other times

Johnny would be found wandering by the police. Usually, he'd somehow avoid arrest.

Johnny's biggest problem was the periodic day off he'd get between shows. June and Marshall grew to dread such days because invariably Johnny would get a supply of pills to take on the road with him and then all hell would be let loose. Even on show days his professionalism was faltering. One night in Waterloo, Iowa, Johnny fell asleep before a show and Marshall was not able to wake him up; yet more evidence of Johnny's terrible state of health.

Some expected June Carter to do more to help Johnny. But she had enough problems on her mind at that time. She was so ashamed about the disastrous state of her second marriage that, for six months after the break-up with her husband, she kept it a secret, even from her beloved mother Maybelle. To make matters worse, her love for Johnny and the guilt it caused was tearing her apart.

In an effort to surround himself with shoulders to cry on in his time of need, Johnny persuaded his old friend Carl Perkins to join his troupe. But Carl had his own problems: he had become a sodden alcoholic who'd just been through a near-fatal auto accident as well as a couple of other disasters. Johnny believed the steady work might help Carl shape up. Instead, in the tour bus the two men would scramble to the back, pull the curtains closed and get drunk and high – Carl on whisky and Johnny on pills.

June observed Johnny's latest crisis from a distance, praying that one day both men would sort themselves out. Johnny and Carl were well aware of what was happening, but neither of them had the strength of character to get themselves off the substances that were wrecking their lives.

It took a small-town sheriff and another night in jail to get Johnny Cash to start thinking about making a choice between self-destruction and self-preservation. Cash had been arrested once again, this time in Lafayette, Georgia, on the morning of November 3, 1967. When the pills finally wore off, he was forced to face the harsh realities of his situation. He later admitted he said to himself at the time: 'I don't ever want out of this cell again. I just want to stay here alone and pray that God will forgive me and then let me die because I'm too weak to face everyone that I'll have to face. Knowin' that my family is heartbroken, knowin' that my friends and fans are hurt and disappointed – it's more than I can reconcile with them.'

Cash had earlier been arrested following a complaint the previous afternoon about a prowler out on Missing Ridge Road, south of the Tennessee state line. Sheriff Ralph Jones had dispatched a deputy in a squad car to pick up the man, who was hauled in and booked as a public drunk. The deputy told the sheriff the man thought he was Johnny Cash, but neither of them believed him. Then Jones checked Cash's wallet and discovered the truth. Johnny was wearing boots, jeans and a dungaree jacket and falling all over the place.

'It was right comical,' Jones later recalled. 'I took some pills off him and locked him up. We put him downstairs in one of the back cells and left him there. Johnny looked skinny as a rail at the time.'

Next morning, Sheriff Jones entered Johnny's cell and woke him up. He told the singer to follow him to his desk. Johnny was shocked when the sheriff handed him back his money and pills. 'I'm goin' to give you your money back and your dope because you know better than most people that God gave you a free will to do with yourself whatever you want to do. Now you can throw the pills away or you can take them and go ahead and kill yourself. Whichever one you want to do, Mr Cash, will be all right with me.'

Johnny was astounded. The drugs were illegal and the sheriff was offering them back to him. Why? Then Sheriff Jones explained his attitude: 'It broke my heart when they brought you in here last night. I left the jail and went home to my wife and told her I had Johnny Cash locked up. I almost wanted to resign and walk out because it was such a heartbreakin' thing for me.'

Jones told Cash again to take his pills and get out, reminding him once more that he had the free will to either kill himself or save his own life. Cash walked out of the jail and threw the pills on the ground. His friend Richard McGibony was waiting outside to pick him up. He got in the car and said, 'Richard, I'm goin' back home to Nashville. You'll never see me high on dope any more.'

'Hope you mean it,' replied his new friend.

Johnny Cash had just been given a bigger break than he deserved – and he knew it. He'd expected to be put in jail. He'd been singularly impressed by what the sheriff had said. But did he now have the willpower to kick the habit? Tragically, the moment he got out of that town he went back and got more pills. But that lost night in jail got Cash thinking, although it took a near-fatal accident a few days later to really drive home the point.

Braxton Dixon – previous owner of Johnny's home in the

countryside outside Nashville – visited that same house on Old Hickory Lake about nine o'clock one chilly morning and noticed Johnny's black Cadillac parked under the carport. He went into the house but couldn't find the singer anywhere.

Then, as he walked away from the house, he saw across the lake that Cash's tractor had tumbled down the bluff and was under water. Braxton rushed down to the lakeside fully expecting to find his friend drowned underneath the tractor. He spotted Cash in a black leather coat stiff with freezing water, his arms wrapped around a tree. Cash had ice on his tousled hair, and his face had turned blue. He had jumped clear just as the tractor hit the water, but he could not summon up the strength to reach the house. The pills had left him too weak. In another half an hour, Braxton estimated, he would have frozen to death.

Though Braxton was a much smaller man, he managed to drag Johnny up. Cash refused to go to his friend's home because he did not want his children to see him in such a dreadful state. Then he insisted on walking to the bluff before returning to his house. He went down, turned over a rock and uncovered a handful of pills he'd hidden there. Even in his near-to-death state he still needed more.

A few minutes later, June Carter called at the house and all hell broke lose. She panicked and screamed at the sight of Johnny and the doctor was called. June felt incensed, betrayed and bewildered; she slapped Johnny hard and then screamed at him. June felt this was the end of the road in terms of her relationship with Johnny. She was going to walk away. Johnny Cash looked stunned. He knew it was a make-or-break moment. He begged June to contact Nat Winston, the Tennessee Commissioner of Mental Health, and ask for his help. When she told him that the Commissioner could not come by until the following day, Cash started to feel desperate for more pills – at which point he collapsed.

When Johnny Cash awoke the next morning in his bed, Nat Winston was sitting next to him. He regarded Cash without a smile and told him, 'Get ready for the fight of your life.' Then he added, 'I'll have to treat you as if you're not responsible, as if you're a child.'

Johnny Cash nodded weakly. He knew he had no choice ...

12

JOHNNY AND JUNE

The late Sixties ushered in the beginnings of the drug culture as we know it today – grass, hash and LSD. Psychedelic posters. Black lights in dormitories. Jimi Hendrix and Janis Joplin (two early casualties of the rock'n'roll lifestyle). Booze just wasn't enough any more. Kids wanted to be different from their parents and get high or trip. But it all boiled down to the same old thing – a means of escape from dull, everyday reality – although the youth of America didn't quite see it that way. Their newest idols – The Beatles, The Rolling Stones – used drugs, sang about drugs and helped popularise their use. Drugs became commonplace. Some parents, even cops and politicians, lit up a joint occasionally. Few realised the full extent of the nightmare they were encouraging. Except perhaps Johnny Cash. While many young Americans were embracing the possibilities awakened by these exciting, dangerous substances, Johnny Cash was about to begin his long journey away from them.

Tennessee Commissioner of Mental Health Nat Winston insisted the only way Johnny Cash could stay alive was if someone went out to his big house near Hendersonville and 'kept the wrong crowd out'. June wasn't sure if she was the person to do that. But when she asked her father he told her she had no choice. 'Pack your suitcase and Maybelle and I will go, too,' he told her.

June was initially reluctant to stay at the house because she was not even officially dating Cash. But Dr Winston told her: 'To hell with what society thinks.' He wanted her to be there and told her she was probably Johnny's only chance of survival. There were no extra beds in the bare-boarded house, so neighbours the Dixons dragged in some mattresses and blankets, which they spread out in the dining room. Maybelle and Anna Dixon did the cooking and everyone took turns keeping vigil with Cash as he began his withdrawal.

It was to be a long haul back to sanity for Johnny Cash. June and her parents and various trusted friends took turns keeping a 24-hour watch on the singer to make sure he swallowed nothing illicit and encountered no one who might tempt him back on to that self-destructive path. Cold turkey was starting for Johnny Cash and he was going to need all the help he could get. June phoned Carl Perkins and Fluke Holland and they started driving over from Jackson regularly. Other friends volunteered to stay at the house with Johnny.

One night, one of 'the wrong crowd' tried to force his way into the house. Neighbour Anna Dixon pulled a kitchen knife on the man and forced him back into his car. It was no easy ride for Johnny Cash. Dr Nat Winston came by the house every day for the first thirty days and Johnny later recalled that he looked forward to those visits because they gave him the courage to fight on. Winston estimated the first stage of Cash's withdrawal would take ten days. He genuinely believed that Johnny might die if he stopped all the drugs immediately, so June provided the pills in decreasing doses, according to the doctor's very precise directions.

Within two days, Johnny stopped taking amphetamines entirely. Winston hadn't wanted him off them so fast because he feared that Cash's vascular system might collapse. With the tranquillisers Equanil it was a more gradual process – twenty for two days, and then fifteen, then ten and then five. These tranquillisers, which created the real physical dependency, gave Cash the worst withdrawal pains. He later described them as 'the ragin', screamin' terrors'. Cash's friends stood by to cook and help, but during the long nights the singer felt more alone than ever before.

For the first time in his life, Johnny Cash was experiencing the real terrors of coming off drugs. He'd always preferred to refer to himself as 'habituated' rather than 'addicted', but it boiled down to the same thing. Johnny suffered appalling nightmares every night for the first ten days of his recovery. Then he'd be left with terrible stomach cramps, which woke him up over and over again.

Cash later recalled: 'All of a sudden a glass ball would begin to expand in my stomach. My eyes were closed, but I could see it. It would grow to the size of a baseball, a volleyball, then a basketball. And about the time I felt that ball was twice the size of a basketball, it lifted me up off the bed. It was a livin' hell.'

Johnny dreamed he was being sucked up through a hole in the roof of the house. Sometimes glass would pierce out of his skin and the corners of his eyes. He'd be pulling splinters of wood and briars and thorns out of his flesh, and sometimes even worms. In his dream he wanted to scream, but he couldn't. He would sit bolt upright in the middle of the night and start pulling drawers out of dressers. Often he'd even turn the bed over, tear up the bedroom and pull up the carpet before ripping down the curtains. Then he'd feel around the edge of the windows, even tearing down the cornices, all because he was desperate to find some pills that he might have left hidden somewhere over the previous years. Thankfully, he never found any.

A few days after his initial incarceration, Cash caught a glance from June looking down at him as he lay in his bed. She wore a quizzical expression and Johnny immediately knew what she was thinking.

'Don't give up on me. I'm gonna win,' he told her emphatically.

Meanwhile, word had got around some music circles that Johnny Cash was finished, that he'd never again perform live on a stage. Few believed the claims that Johnny was reforming or changing for the better, because they'd all heard it before. However, those closest to Cash believed those changes were happening. The Statler Brothers, The Carter Family, Luther Perkins, Marshall Grant and Fluke Holland all remained convinced that Johnny was on the road to recovery. Within two months, Cash was eating reasonably well and anxious to get back to a 'normal' life, if you could apply that description to the life of a living legend of country music.

A live appearance soon followed. Johnny Cash was astonished to find crowds still packing in to see him. He was absolutely convinced there was only one person in the world who was responsible for his recovery: June Carter. He believed she was the only person who truly understood his complex nature. So it was hardly surprising when he asked her to marry him.

Johnny Cash's proposal to June Carter was not made at a remote table by candlelight or on bended knee. Cash actually asked June for her hand in marriage while onstage in London, Ontario, in front of five thousand paying fans. June looked at him in disbelief and quietly suggested that they go on with the show. Then she turned to her mother Maybelle Carter and begged her to play a song. But she flatly refused – so June frantically turned to the other performers to bail her out. The audience, meanwhile, demanded an answer, calling out, 'Say yes! Say yes!' Finally, June, with a slight smile crossing her face, said, 'All right. Yes I will.'

But there was a hidden agenda behind Johnny's very public decision to marry June. He'd been clean and sober for over three months and had even reconciled with God and his family. He was being urged to perform fresh dates at venues he'd cancelled due to his drug and drink problems over the previous few years. This was going to be the beginning of a new life.

Johnny recorded a second concert at California's Folsom

Prison on February 10, 1968. His earlier concert at the jail had been instigated by his friend the Rev Gressett, who'd asked Johnny to perform in 1966 on behalf of all the inmates he'd counselled over the years. That concert had been such a success that Johnny spent the following two years talking about the possibility of recording an album in a prison. That decision led to him making what was to be one of his most successful albums: *Johnny Cash – Live at Folsom Prison*. Folsom had always been an enigma to Johnny, who had written the song 'Folsom Prison Blues' after seeing a documentary on the prison in a movie theatre back in the mid-Fifties. The song had been released in 1955 to moderate acclaim, but the new live version soared straight to number one in the country charts.

Having stopped taking pills, Johnny was now better able to put his ideas into motion and actually follow through on them. The MC for the Folsom show was Hugh Cherry, an old friend of Johnny's from Los Angeles. He warmed up the audience superbly and even introduced Johnny's father Ray. Cherry also made a very special request to the audience, 'When Johnny Cash comes out, don't applaud, please. Let him introduce himself then react naturally.' A few moments later, Johnny stepped up to the microphone, said, 'Hello, I'm Johnny Cash', and Luther Perkins kicked off 'Folsom Prison Blues'. Thus began a slice of recording history. The album went on to sell almost six million copies, and the single record sold another two million.

The show at Folsom went off without a hitch. The prisoners were returned to their cells, and Johnny and his troupe boarded the bus to leave for the motel. Johnny later recalled that he turned to June and told her, 'I have a feeling that lots of good things are beginnin' to happen to us.'

A few days later, Johnny and June won a Grammy for their first ever duet, on 'Jackson'. At the ceremony, Johnny conceded that the award would make a 'nice wedding present'. The assumption around Nashville was that June Carter had got Johnny Cash off pills and they'd all live happily ever after.

When Johnny and June went up to accept their award there was initially a stunned silence from the audience. After all, this was the man who was rumoured to be at death's door due to his addiction to pills. Then everyone sprang to their feet and applauded for five full minutes. It seemed these people had been rooting for Johnny Cash for a long time and they all acknowledged that standing by his side during those trying months had been a girl they all knew and loved, one of their very own.

Johnny Cash and June Carter were married on March 1, 1968, at a church in Franklin, Kentucky, just north of Nashville. There were hundreds of relatives, friends and musicians in attendance at the reception, held at Johnny's enormous Lakeside home. Merle Kilgore – who'd written 'Ring of Fire' with June – was Johnny's best man and proved to be the life and soul of the party after the ceremony. There was no alcohol served, and Johnny later insisted that everyone present must have been high on life! One of their Nashville friends summed up the feelings of all who knew the happy couple when he said, 'Johnny's got a miracle pulling for him, and that's June Carter!'

Despite all the praise for June, Johnny's doctor Nat

Winston proclaimed it was the singer himself who'd managed to beat his demons. He'd never seen anyone come off pills with the guts that Johnny had showed. The doctor knew that relapses were entirely possible, but he was convinced Johnny had made it through the worst.

Cash knew that many people had written him off as a drug-addicted mess. They'd acted as if they were proud of him when he beat the pills, but he believed that many in the country music business were still bitter about what he'd done. Cash reckoned many of them would have liked him to go ahead and die and then they'd have had a legend to sing about. 'They'd have put me in hillbilly heaven,' he said years later.

June later perfectly summed up the way she felt about Johnny in her best-selling 1987 autobiographical book *From The Heart*. A rather unusual book in its presentation and style, her love for Johnny nevertheless came through loud and clear, as is evident in the following excerpt:

> *My husband's name is John R. John for first. R for Rah (Hurrah), R-Rajah-(King of country); R-ramrod (of his family), R-Rasputin (sometimes a holy term), and R for really Cash; R for Rich – a little rich; R for ready – for that he always is, ready. John Ready Cash – ready – first in faith, and ready to love and defend his family, of which there is a pretty good group.*

It was an extraordinary testament to the love June felt for her man, a subject that she kept coming back proudly to throughout the book.

Soon after their marriage, the couple left for a tour of Europe. Some said they were stuck together like glue; June was determined not to leave Johnny for a second of solitude for fear he might slide back into reliance on drink and drugs. In Europe, they visited a host of cities, including Frankfurt, Munich, Hamburg, Glasgow, London, Dublin and Manchester. It was a gruelling schedule, but they gave each other the strength to get through it all.

After the tour, June and Johnny went on vacation to Israel, where they visited historic and religious sites. But just days after their return to the US, devastating news reached them: troupe member Luther Perkins had perished in a fire in his home. Johnny was stunned. Luther had been his right-hand man through all the good and bad times. For a few days, he even wondered whether he could carry on without his great friend. His army of advisers desperately wanted the Johnny Cash roadshow out again, but the singer refused steadfastly to replace Luther.

'How can we even think about going on without him,' Johnny kept saying over and over again, exploding angrily when anyone suggested he had no choice. Carl Perkins filled in as lead guitarist for the following two months, but Luther's death left a dark shadow over the stage show.

Eventually, after much soul searching, Johnny gave in to the inevitable pressure and replaced Luther with a young musician named Bob Wootten, who reminded Johnny of himself in his earlier years. Wootten could play every song of Cash's exactly as it had been recorded; he seemed a natural choice.

Johnny Cash always had a fascination for gadgets and his

fellow band members were astonished when he gratefully accepted a watch as a gift from Marshall Grant – and then proceeded to do everything in his power to destroy it. Marshall had promised Johnny the watch was guaranteed waterproof and shockproof when he gave it to the singer and Johnny decided to put it to *all* the tests. He dunked it in his Coke at driving stops. He submerged it in his coffee at breakfast. He thumped it against coffee-shop tables, even dropped it out of a few hotel windows. Home from tour, he froze it in his refrigerator, boiled it on the stove and towed it behind his motorboat. The watch kept ticking. Before he could deliver the ultimate coup de grace, it was (mercifully) stolen from his Michigan hotel room.

Johnny had by now stayed off the drugs and booze for long period of time, mainly thanks to his settled family life and June's presence at his side. Johnny knew only too well that the 'old demon deception' was still perched on his shoulder, waiting for the perfect opportunity to slide back into his life. That opportunity would come – thanks to the war in Vietnam.

Johnny was a great patriot, fervently believed in the United States defending itself and others, and had no sympathy for draft dodgers, unpatriotic or unsupportive folk. For that reason he didn't hesitate to travel to Vietnam with June and the rest of The Johnny Cash Show to play nightclubs, barracks and even the occasional hospital room. He looked on it as his patriotic duty.

Stopping over in Okinawa en route to Vietnam, Johnny and his troupe did two shows a night and also visited military hospitals for the occasional singalong. June took dozens of wounded servicemen's names and home phone numbers with the promise that she'd call their folks when she got back home. Later, when they made it back to the States, June kept to her pledge and spent two days solidly on the phone.

But back in Okinawa, Johnny was exhausted by the gruelling programme and fell seriously ill with a fever before the troupe took off for their next stop in Manila. After two more shows, a doctor was called in to examine Cash, who was sweating profusely. Part of it was caused by his fever, but Johnny also knew he was weakening in other ways.

'Can't you gimme somethin' I can take to help me through the next few shows, doc?'

'Dexedrine or Dexamyl?' came the reply.

Johnny watched as the doctor placed the pills on his bedside table. At that moment he knew he'd lost the biggest battle of his life.

By the time Cash and his troupe landed in Vietnam, Johnny was flying as high as a kite. That handful of tablets was enough for the demons to step back in and enter his head. At first, he believed he'd keep his vice secret from all around him. He looked at his eyes in the mirror and they didn't seem too dilated. No one would notice, or so he thought.

But, within days, Johnny was also mixing vast quantities of the drugs with neat brandy. June immediately knew what was happening and tried to make Johnny calm down because she knew that the more nervous he got the more he'd increase his consumption of pills.

Johnny later summed up his drug-induced dilemma: 'The devil was way ahead in this round of my life's battle. June knew what was the matter. I knew she knew. She sat in a corner, head down. I'd call a waiter and tell him, "Bring me a double shot of brandy. I've got to clear my throat." June turned pale. She walked over and whispered to me, "Oh, no, John. Not brandy mixed with whatever you've already taken. You know what it'll do to you."

'"Mind your own business," I said, gulping the brandy down. "I've got a show to do."'

And so it went on. Johnny was soon consuming drugs on virtually an hourly basis and still trying to fulfil every date on the tour of Vietnam. Not surprisingly, he reached the point where he couldn't actually sing. Johnny never forgot one appearance in front of thousands of servicemen. He later recalled: 'I stood in one spot to keep from falling on my face and whispered my songs. After an hour of that hell, I closed the show with, "I'm sorry I was in such bad shape. You'll never see me this way again." And then I walked off.'

That night, Johnny returned to a self-inflicted cold turkey. He later said he couldn't lie still. His skin was crawling, muscle spasms twisted and tortured his back and neck. Finally, June called the hotel doctor – a different one this time – who gave Cash a shot to put him to sleep. The following day, Johnny stuffed his few remaining tablets down the side of a couch in his hotel room, intending to leave them behind. For four days and nights he did not touch them. But then, just before the troupe was due to leave for Tokyo, Johnny reached down the side of that couch and took the pills out.

Once in Japan, he stumbled through more concerts, consuming yet more tablets by the handful. Back in their hotel the night before departure for the US, June confronted her husband yet again. Johnny confessed to everything and the couple leaned by the side of the bed and prayed.

The following morning, Johnny flushed the last of his drugs down the toilet and prayed for yet another chance to return to a clean life.

• • • •

Another thing happened to Cash while he was in Vietnam. He began to distance himself from his previously gung-ho attitudes towards American-involved conflicts. One night at the Long Blinh air base, a Pima Indian marine came up to the stage while Johnny was singing 'The Ballard of Ira Hayes'. At the end of the song, the young Native American asked Johnny to take his beer and, with tears running down his chin, he told the singer, 'I may die tomorrow but I want you to know that I ain't never been so alive as I am tonight.' Johnny later admitted he felt a strange combination of emotions when he heard that young man. He wanted to give his boys all the support they deserved, but he also knew that most of them did not even want to be there in the first place. Afterwards, Cash dubbed himself a 'dove with claws', because he felt so confused about the entire war issue.

After Johnny's return home from Asia, he was even more torn about his politics. He still believed every man should serve his country, but he couldn't agree with the atrocities taking place in Vietnam. Wife June was puzzled by her husband's attitudes. She later explained: 'John's not left and he's not right. He once said to me, "Don't ask me what I think about anything unless you want to know about the next five minutes. My mind changes all the time. I believe one thing one month and the next month I believe something else. I'm changing. I'm growing. I'm becoming."'

Maybe that was Johnny's biggest problem in life ...

13

ON TOP

June and Johnny lived in complete and utter wedded bliss once he'd shaken off that temporary 'setback' with drugs in the Far East. The couple never discussed it with the others in the troupe because they feared it might ruin morale if it was known Cash had fallen off the rails so quickly after his initial recovery. Johnny was convinced it would also give undue recognition to the dark and negative forces that had so nearly destroyed him. He simply had to move on.

Life at the house by the lake near Hendersonville actually became idyllic for the first time. June's children Carlene and Rosey adored the countryside and Johnny's daughters were able to come and visit any time they wanted. Across the street stood a large house built specifically for Johnny's parents. Inside his own house, a kitchen disappeared into a row of closets; the bedroom balcony looked out on Old

Hickory Lake, which was full of bass and crappie. A genuine impression of peace and tranquillity was there for all to see.

The house with its round glass-walled bedroom and rustic-elegant living room even had its own display shelf containing a cluster of cotton on a stalk. It was cotton from Dyess, Arkansas – a little shrine to childhood hard times. Cash also had a dock built on the lake for his own speedboat, which was frequently used for water-skiing and fishing boats. Sometimes, guests such as Bob Dylan would appear and hang out for a weekend.

One time, Cash and Dylan wrote a song together called 'Wanted Man' as they sat at the dock fishing and eating lunch. Johnny Cash later told a friend the two musical megastars were so interested in fishing they rushed the song so they could get back to their fishing lines.

Bob Dylan became a very special friend to Johnny during this period and Cash described him as 'probably the greatest poet of our times'. Johnny also wrote a tribute to Dylan published in the Bob Dylan songbook of the album *Nashville Skyline*. Johnny's poem was a free-verse piece titled 'Of Bob Dylan'.

Other times, Cash and Dylan sat up all night, singing and playing each other's songs, or any other tune that took their fancy. At dawn, they'd delay going to bed until they'd been out on the lake together to match wits with some early biting fish. Johnny Cash reckoned he got true inspiration from people such as Bob Dylan. 'It's like I hear something they've written and think to myself, Why couldn't I write that – that's the way I think too. Maybe it's more like a challenge than an inspiration.'

Despite the passing years, Johnny Cash still felt an overwhelming guilt about his tragic brother Jack. It had been more than twenty years since he'd died, but Johnny couldn't get him out of his mind. He steadfastly refused to sing any of the songs that were sung at Jack's funeral. He even vowed that ten per cent of all his songs would always be sacred ones, and dedicated an album to Jack, *The Holy Land*, which revolved around the trip to Jerusalem and the sacred sites of Christianity.

Johnny Cash's continuing relationship with God was a desperate effort to stay in touch with brother Jack. To make sure that he was never forgotten. Johnny genuinely believed (and did until his dying day) that eventually the two would meet in heaven and carry on where they left off. No one will know if that dream ever came true, but it was a starting point for Johnny's revived commitment to God. He saw himself on a mission to bring everyone together in peace and harmony. He believed his own superstardom helped him to be the ultimate messenger and even gave him certain powers. Sometimes, those powers led him to believe he was invincible and that was when trouble brewed. On other occasions, he simply tried to channel them in the right direction.

As well as Bob Dylan being a regular visitor to the house, there were a vast number of other big names living in the Hendersonville neighbourhood by this time. At the local Baptist ministry every Sunday, famous worshippers included Roy Orbison, Kris Kristofferson and Skeeter Davis. A sign would regularly appear at the lynch-gate warning 'Absolutely No Autographs or Pictures Taken Inside This Sanctuary'.

On the recording side of things, Johnny found himself

with one of his biggest ever hit after 'Daddy Sang Bass' was released on January 4, 1969. June's support was vital in the making of the song, which was written by Carl Perkins. That same year, Johnny and June also conceived a child while they were in the glamorous Virgin Islands. It was a beautiful vacation. Hot, sunny days on the beach and in the surf; then at night the moonlight filtered through the palm trees and worked its magic. June getting pregnant seemed the perfect way to round it off.

Around this time, Columbia Records asked Johnny to record another album in a prison, and this time a concert was arranged in notorious San Quentin, California. Don Davis, a Nashville music publisher, called Johnny the day before he was due to travel to San Quentin and begged him to consider trying out a new song he'd just acquired.

'It's called "A Boy Named Sue",' explained Davis enthusiastically.

Johnny didn't question the oddball title and told Davis to get the song's author Shel Silverstein to come out to the lake and play it to him. What he did not tell David or Silverstein was that he was planning a guitar pull party at his mansion that evening. Guests included Bob Dylan, singing 'Lay Lady, Lay', Graham Nash belting out 'Marrakesh Express', Joni Mitchell singing 'Both Sides Now', Kris Kristofferson with 'Me and Bobby McGee'... and then Shel Silverstein singing 'A Boy Named Sue'. The moment Johnny Cash heard it, he knew that Davis was right about the song. But he had so much on his mind, because he was about to leave for San Quentin, that he didn't have time to learn the lyrics.

Thus it was that, at San Quentin, Johnny laid the lyrics on

the floor in front of him and read them off, one time through with no rehearsal. And so was born probably the most famous song he ever performed. 'A Boy Named Sue' and the San Quentin album surpassed the success of *Folsom Prison*, making Johnny Cash Columbia Records' biggest-selling artist in 1969, with over six million albums sold plus half that many single records.

During the San Quentin recording, Johnny shocked some of his more straight-laced fans by using a profanity – 'son of a bitch'. It was later bleeped out. Johnny's 'bad language' got a lot of coverage in the press; Johnny himself was annoyed that he'd let it slip out and later blamed the entire situation on the fact that his bad old ways had still not been completely shaken off – and actually never would. Johnny's attitude towards convicts always remained the same. He believed that the airwaves belonged to everybody – after all, anybody could turn on a radio. So he felt prisoners deserved the same musical choices as the rest of the population.

But there was a hidden agenda behind Johnny's prison concerts. He was appalled by the poor conditions inside so many jails across America and felt that anything which brought that to the public attention was worthwhile. 'I don't see anything good comin' out of prison. You put men in like animals and tear the souls and guts out of them – and let them out worse than when they came in.'

Johnny believed that the prison system was just a school for crime. Prisons were also seriously overcrowded, often with not enough staff to run them at night. He was shocked that many prisons did not even have a doctor on call at night. He also couldn't understand why marijuana smokers were being locked in cells with murderers and bank robbers. Prison was supposed to help a man to improve his life, not make it worse, Cash later argued. The whole system sucked and the only way Johnny believed he could make a difference was through his songs.

Years later he explained: 'How can it work? How could this torment possibly do anybody any good ... You sit on your cold steel mattressless bunk and watch a cockroach crawl out from under the filthy toilet, and you don't kill it. You envy the roach his freedom as you watch it crawl out under the cell door.'

Johnny liked to see convicts laugh because 'I know how lonely they are.' His speciality was scrawling down a song for a particular prison just before he arrived there. Once, at Arkansas Cummins Prison Farm, the scene of barbaric practices in the past and still no model of penology, he lectured the State Legislator in song: 'There's a lot of things that need changing, Mr Legislator Man,' he belted out, eyeing a group of lawmakers present. The appearance was being televised and Cash implored the 'fat, rich Arkansas farmers' in the audience to give liberally to funds for a prison chapel. He revealed he was giving $5,000 and then that Governor Winthrop Rockefeller had given $10,000, 'but he can afford it'. Near the end of the programme, the Prisons Commissioner came on stage and said that Johnny had said 'some things I've been afraid to say' in his song. 'That's all right,' replied Johnny. 'I had nothing to lose.' As Johnny's good friend the ex-convict Merle Haggard said of the star, 'Johnny Cash understands what it's like to be in prison, but he doesn't know ...'

The San Quentin recording of 'A Boy Named Sue' was certified a million seller on August 14, 1969. Nine days later, it ascended to number one on the *Billboard* country chart, peaking that same week at number two on the pop chart – just behind The Rolling Stones' 'Honky Tonk Women'.

• • • •

The 1969 Country Music Association Awards show belonged almost exclusively to Johnny Cash. He was named Entertainer of the Year, male Vocalist of the Year and (along with June Carter) Vocal Group of the Year. *Johnny Cash at San Quentin* brought him his second straight Album of the Year award and 'A Boy Named Sue' earned Single of the Year. Along with Glen Campbell, television had made Johnny the most recognisable country performer of that or any era.

In the late summer of 1969, Johnny agreed to star in his own TV show on the ABC network. *The Johnny Cash Show* was to be a blend of old-time country/hillbilly singing, interesting and unusual guests (including Bob Dylan) plus a little preaching by 'Reverend' Johnny Cash and a bucketload of good music. The show proved an instant hit and ran for three years, frequently holding the top spots on the charts with an estimated 23 million viewers each week. Cash was particularly proud of the appearances of Merle Haggard and Charley Pride, who went on to make it big following their exposure on his show.

The first full year of the programme proved an immensely enjoyable experience for Johnny Cash. He later recalled: 'Being in America's living room every week via TV, singing songs I felt were right for me, songs I believed my audience wanted to hear. I was talking to the heart of my audience through hymns and the "Ride This Train" segment. I became, in many ways, public property.'

One of Johnny's guests on the show was Mike Nesmith of The Monkees, who put Cash right on the spot about how all this TV fame would affect his marriage. 'So now you're a superstar, John. Want to make a bet on how long your marriage will last, how long you'll have this beautiful home?'

Nesmith's cheeky challenge greatly disturbed Cash.

'Why shouldn't it last?' he asked the chart-topping pop star.

'Fame is fleeting and, when it flies, it takes the trappings with it.'

Johnny knew exactly what Nesmith meant and later admitted he never forgot those words.

Meanwhile, as is so often the case with television, *The Johnny Cash Show* gradually started to represent a relentless treadmill for Johnny Cash following that first successful season. Cash blew a gasket when the producers cancelled the 'Ride This Train' segment that featured a weekly imaginary train ride to a particular time and place in US history. TV bosses also began insisting Johnny welcome cabaret and café society celebrities on board his train. It wasn't what he had intended.

'I couldn't do what I wanted to do, because the sponsor was the real star,' Johnny later recalled.

Shortly afterwards, they cancelled the programme. Cash later looked back on those experiences in Hollywood as yet another example of him being treated like a piece of merchandise by the TV network, a cog in their wheel, and when the wheel started squeaking and wobbling they happily chopped him down like a rotting oak tree.

Johnny particularly loathed the way every part of his personal and family life was exploited by his appearances on TV. He felt as if the show's executives, writers and directors were all trying to steal his soul. He even believed their only goal was good ratings and eventually he'd started walking round the studio thinking to himself, I don't have to do this. What am I doing this for?

Despite his inner reservations, Cash agreed to act in a new TV drama series, which he presumed wouldn't have the same problems. He played a character called John Andrew Jackson, a country boy who'd been through Vanderbilt Law School and become a detective in the Nashville Police Department. In fact, Johnny was playing Johnny as a policeman. His character had even, rather conveniently, always wanted to be a singer, and the Nashville music scene provided the backdrop to the show.

Hollywood presumed that Johnny was determined to prove himself as an actor, although Johnny later insisted to friends he had no such intentions. He protested that he'd always love music much more than acting, but was realistic enough to realise he was essentially playing himself in the series – so it wasn't like real acting.

Johnny made a number of *Johnny Cash Christmas Specials* in the early Seventies. Most of them were sugary affairs deliberately aimed at a mainstream Middle American audience rather than hardened country buffs. Johnny was expected to jam along with all sorts of different kinds of musicians, some of whom he didn't always have the greatest respect for. So it was ironic that an encounter with one of Cash's oldest musical associates, Jerry Lee Lewis, created more friction than anything else during the making of these programmes. Problems were sparked when Jerry Lee insisted on referring to himself in the third person, resulting in the memorable line, 'I'm dreaming of a white Christmas/just like the ones old Killer used to know' in Irving Berlin's classic yuletide song.

Johnny and the show's producers were infuriated and they certainly didn't see the funny side of it. Jerry Lee refused to toe the line, however, and in the end his section of the show was edited out. This caused a major rift between the two stars that never really healed properly, despite a reunion of sorts more than fifteen years later.

Meanwhile, Johnny Cash still had one bizarre secret acting ambition that he harboured with great enthusiasm – to one day play the apostle Paul. He later explained: 'He was beaten. He was shipwrecked. He was boiled in oil. Five times the Romans gave him 39 lashes. He had his ribs broken, his legs broken and he was put on the rack. He was stoned three times, left for dead twice. All this while he went round Asia and Europe establishing churches. And, despite the persecution, he returned to each church, again and again, to make sure it was still running. He was taken prisoner in Rome, and released because he was a Roman citizen. He gained favour with Caesar, who let him live in the palace, where he promptly converted the workers. He was finally beheaded by Nero, who decided he needed somebody to blame for the plight of Rome. What impressed me about Paul is that during all this he said, "I have learned through Christ that I can be satisfied in whatever state I'm in."' Johnny Cash had been through his own kind of hell, his mind boiled in barbiturates, his lows signified by the black he continued to wear. To say he could relate to the suffering of the apostle Paul might have been something of an understatement.

And still everyone wanted a piece of their hero. What bothered the star was where would it all end? He sometimes felt as if he was being stretched to bursting point. Many fans apparently turned to him as if he could somehow solve the troubles of the world. One time he heard about a man in Nashville fatally ill with a kidney disease so, though he'd never met him, he secretly sent him $10,000 for an artificial kidney machine. Initially, Cash's donation was budgeted for operating expenses until Johnny complained and the sick man – who was black as well as poor – got his life-saving equipment. Johnny summed up his dilemma as thus: 'If I do help them all, there will be others. I don't know what to do with all this power. I keep searchin' for wisdom, hopin' I'll say the right thing and do the right thing.' Cash was starting to feel that so many people were chasing him and trying to use him for their own personal reasons that he'd rather just get rid of all the money and stick to what he knew best – singing.

In the final weeks of 1969, new wife June was booked into the Seventh Day Adventist Hospital in Madison, Tennessee, for the delivery of the couple's first child. Ironically, the doctor who was to attend the birth was Dr Frederec Cothren, who'd counselled Johnny about his drug problems three years earlier. Cothren didn't hold those earlier problems against Cash so he was more than happy to attend the birth of the couple's son, which, unfortunately, the star missed because he was appearing on *The Grand Ole Opry* at the time – having been allowed back in on the assumption that his hard-living days were over.

Baby John Carter Cash helped fill a void in Johnny's marriage. Both he and June knew only too well that their relationship could be in trouble if they didn't stay and work together. The birth of Johnny's one and only son definitely resealed the bond of their marriage and reminded Johnny just how much he needed June. There had been times during both his marriages when Johnny had allowed the hangers-on and the pedlars to rule his life, but he always knew that June would be there in the background keeping an eye on him, making sure that this time he stayed on the straight and narrow. As Cash later recalled: 'I was never really whole without her, never really felt like a concert was complete without her.'

Ironically, it was June's absence from the shows during the later stages of her pregnancy that had really driven the message home to Johnny loud and clear. The couple regularly talked about the price they'd both paid for his fame. They spoke of the ups and downs, the good times and the bad, the heartbreak and the victories, and all of that helped them stay together. Now this new child had come along and presented Johnny with a new chance to make up for all that time he'd missed with his daughters.

The couple decided they'd take John Carter Cash with them on every tour, which meant finding someone very special to look after the boy. Within hours of their son's birth they'd recruited a little nurse named Winafred Kelley who immediately became part of the Cash family.

By 1970, Johnny's income had sky-rocketed to four million dollars per year. His record sales remained phenomenal, topping a staggering fifteen million at that point. Columbia – the largest record company in the world at the time – revealed that Johnny was number three among its best-selling artists, trailing only Barbra Streisand and Johnny Mathis. But time remained Johnny's enemy. There'd never be enough time to do half the things he wanted to do, like going fishing with his father, which they managed only rarely.

On the land surrounding Cash's vast house near Hendersonville, he managed to put aside an acre of land for a vegetable garden, which became his private sanctuary. It was his escape valve when he went to work off the pressures of his career and the headaches from the complex web of corporations that had taken over his business affairs.

Yet, despite all the money and fame, Johnny Cash still knew that hard work was the keystone to his life. He was born and bred to it and, in the final analysis, the changes in that condition since he chopped cotton on his father's acres of delta land in Dyess, Arkansas, were purely technical. Publicly, Cash insisted to his adoring public that he was 'so damned happy I could bust. I'm havin' a ball!' But secretly he harboured ambitions of an entirely different nature from showbusiness success. He wanted to make more time for himself and his family because he didn't want to make the same sort of mistakes he'd made all those years earlier. Was that really asking too much?

In 1970, Johnny Cash was invited to perform at the White House for President Richard M Nixon. Nixon claimed to be a big fan of Johnny's – not just for his music, but also for the principles and moral reputation of the singer. It was even rumoured that right-wing Nixon had requested Cash to perform several specific songs. Johnny Cash might have cleaned up and sobered up by this time, but he could still be as characteristically obstinate as ever and he refused point blank to perform two of the songs requested by the President. They were 'Okie From Muskogee' and 'Welfare Cadillac'. Cash later claimed they were condescending and defamatory tunes. In any case, they were not part of his repertoire.

The resulting 'snub' by Johnny to the most powerful leader in the Western world was splashed across US newspapers and television. A barrage of reporters eventually surrounded Johnny at his hotel when the news slipped out. But Cash was unrepentant. There was no way he would play those songs. In the end Nixon had to make do with other songs from the Cash catalogue, including 'A Boy Named Sue' and 'Folsom Prison Blues'. After the concert, Johnny and June spent an hour with the Nixons and not one word was mentioned about Johnny's 'snub'.

Not long after this, the scandal of Watergate blew up and Johnny got his 'revenge' when he decided to pop in and watch the trial of Haldeman, Ehrlichman and the rest of the so-called Watergate 'burglars'. The singer had been travelling back from an afternoon with his friend Billy Graham in Norfolk, Virginia, when he decided to turn up at the section of the trial that featured the tape of Nixon talking about a cover-up to Haldeman.

Haldeman's jaw dropped open at the sight of the singing star strolling into court. He immediately turned to someone else and then looked back at Johnny with an expression on his face that seemed to ask, 'What the hell is he doing here?' When the court took a recess, Johnny walked over to Haldeman, introduced himself and told him, 'Wait a minute, I'm not on any side. I'm here as a spectator. You're a piece of American history, whether you like it or not, and I'm just here to witness it.'

Haldeman asked if Johnny would have a cup of coffee with him during the next recess. The singer and June went out with him and Ehrlichman, who said nothing other than hello. At the table, the first thing Haldeman asked was, 'You've been on the hot seat, haven't you?'

'Sure have,' answered Johnny, who then went on to tell Haldeman about his drug busts.

'You know how it feels, then?' asked Haldeman.

'Yeah, it don't feel good, does it?'

Haldeman then made an extraordinary comment to Johnny Cash: 'I just want you to know that I did what I thought was right at the time. I was only trying to do my job.'

After Haldeman went back to the court, Johnny and June departed. They both later insisted that Haldeman was basically a good man who'd got himself caught up in something he had no control over. That encounter had a profound effect on Johnny's political beliefs. Essentially, he considered himself a committed Christian and that meant understanding the power of forgiveness. Johnny genuinely believed that if he took the words of Jesus literally and applied them to his everyday life then he'd discover the meaning of fulfilment.

In September, 1970, Johnny made yet another appearance on the *Billboard* charts with his latest single, 'Sunday

Morning Coming Down', written by his good friend Kris Kristofferson. Kristofferson had written the song while he was living in a dilapidated tenement building following a divorce. He pitched the song to Johnny after landing in his back yard in a helicopter, falling out of the aircraft with a beer can in one hand and a copy of the song in the other. Kristofferson had been pursuing Johnny for weeks to get him to listen to the song and screamed across his back yard, 'By God, I'm gonna get a song to you one way or another.'

Johnny replied, 'Well, you just did, let's go in and hear it.'

After Johnny cut the song, it remained at number one for two weeks. During that period, the Country Music Association named it Song of the Year.

On April 23, 1970, Johnny gave up smoking. It was a date that would be firmly imprinted on his mind for the rest of his life. Johnny had smoked since he was a teenager and it felt like another version of that awful cold turkey when he went through thirty days of fighting and praying to beat the habit. Cash found himself dreaming of cigarettes and even caught himself inhaling the fumes from the stove in the kitchen of the house in Hendersonville some days. Other times he would find himself looking at the leaves on trees wondering if he could crunch them up and smoke them. After that first thirty days it got a little easier and he felt he'd turned the corner.

Cash developed an appalling cough while trying to give up cigarettes, which took months to go. While he occasionally took a few puffs from time to time, that date April 23, 1970 never left his mind. It was a lasting reminder of the second most important battle of his life.

Later in 1970, Johnny set the all-time record gross for an

appearance in the history of the city of Detroit, Michigan. By today's standards it might seem rather small, but the $131,000 taken at the box office was something to be genuinely proud of. Meanwhile, his latest album, *Hello, I'm Johnny Cash*, was anchored firmly in the number-one spot in the *Billboard* chart. His popularity was undiminished.

In addition to – and perhaps because of – all this commercial success, Cash was starting to get a good head for business. He set up his own house brand and with that came the formation of a number of companies that would give him more freedom with – and profit from – his material.

Around this time, Johnny's baby sister Reba Ann Cash Hancock began working for her brother as a fan club representative. She was rapidly promoted to general manager of both The House of Cash (an ASCAP company) and the The Sound of Cash (a BMI company). These companies would offer Johnny more security in the near future when several lawsuits were expected to emerge, most of them dealing with past due royalties owed to both Johnny and the other members of his band. Sister Reba was a child bride in Arkansas long before Johnny Cash made it in showbusiness. She was also a grandmother in her mid-thirties. And the striking brunette was henceforth going to be on hand to do everything from screening her brother from the press to setting up appointments for various members of his organisation.

There was also the problem of what to do with the thousands of cards and letters that arrived every week. Johnny bought a large building a mile from his home in Hendersonville where sister Reba was based. She hired a staff of people to take care of the mail and public contracts. She organised the building of a recording studio and became Johnny's right arm in most business and personal affairs. Johnny felt safe and secure in the hands of sister Reba, a level-headed lady with an eye for detail and with nothing but Johnny's best interests at heart.

Every week, literally hundreds of requests for appearances came from charities, churches, preachers, prisons, even drug centres. Reba tried to filter out the sensible letters, but often June, Johnny and Reba would stay up half the night trying to sort out all the correspondence.

Over at the main house, hundreds of people flocked to gawp at the Johnny Cash lakeside mansion in tour buses each week. Johnny didn't seem to mind, even when they tried to get him to wave back as he walked across the vast front window to his sitting room.

Johnny's parents Ray and Carrie – back from California and living in the house Johnny had built for them across the lake – had no idea just how popular Johnny had become in the Nashville area. They missed the quiet peaceful life of California – a flood of people were now turning up at their front door, wanting to take pictures or to ask about Johnny. The Cashes were kind and courteous to all the tourists and visitors, posing for photos, signing autographs and answering a million questions, but it disturbed their once-quiet lives to play host to all these intruders.

Back at Johnny's mansion across the lake, the superstar always had to leave the house early for any appointment in order to spend a few minutes meeting the people at his gate. It was a bizarre existence. Only once did Johnny ever lose his temper and that was when he came home one evening and found a strange man standing in his stepdaughter Rosey's bedroom. Rosey had just walked in ahead of her stepfather and was terrified. Johnny stopped in his tracks when he saw the man, who was clearly as nervous as he was.

'I'm not going to hurt you,' the man told Rosey, grinning. Johnny immediately realised he was high on something. He recognised the symptoms only too well.

'Who're you and how d'you get in here?' asked Johnny.

'I slipped in,' laughed the man. 'The door was open. You don't know me.'

Johnny suddenly lurched for the man, grabbed him around the head and ran, dragging him out the door and throwing him into the yard. The man never uttered another word; he simply turned and ran as fast as he could off the property.

'I don't think the Lord sent him,' growled Johnny.

• • • •

In 1974, Johnny held several fundraising events to collect cash for the beleaguered prison system. At the same time, he and his troupe also continued to take on the cause of the American Indian, leading to yet more rumours that he was himself part-Cherokee – part of the Cash mythology that exists to this day. The truth is that Johnny was very partial to Native American legends, embracing the beliefs that honoured a higher power and the possibility of spirits that guided the soul and kept it from danger. It was only natural that someone like Johnny would hope that some of those good spirits might rub off on him.

Contrary to popular legend, Johnny Cash had not spent

time in any federal prisons. He had been so strongly identified with them through his performances at Folsom and San Quentin that people just presumed he was an ex-con. But Johnny's empathy for inmates came from noticing the deplorable conditions in which many prisoners lived and he still continued to make a point of mentioning this whenever he talked to anyone in political office. As a result, Johnny remained the convicts' favourite. He was the guy who fought his way to the top, but never forgot the real people out there, the ones who bought his records and saw him perform.

14

TRIALS AND TRIBULATIONS

The envelope was simple. It was addressed to Johnny Cash and it did not have a postmark. The Man in Black opened it without giving it much thought, but when he began reading the note inside he stopped dead in his tracks: *Put $250,000 in a plain brown paper bag, and drop it at the exit of I-25 and [a street name], if you value the lives of your kids. Do it today.*

Johnny was terrified. He went straight into the kitchen of that huge house near Hendersonville and told June. She staggered back in shock. What about the kids? Were they safe at school? What if something was happening to them at this moment?

'John, I need a gun,' uttered June, unable to think of anything else to say.

'You afraid?' asked Johnny.

'Yes, I'm afraid. But not of this bunch.'

Johnny Cash then hit the phones and started talking to sheriffs, state investigators, even the FBI. Then June got a call on her personal line. It was daughter Carlene, who was at school.

She told June: 'Momma, Rosey called me to ask how you were. Only, Mother, I know my own sister. It wasn't Rosey, Mom, and, by the way, there was a long black limo following me and my date last night. Thought I'd better tell you that, too.'

Just a couple of hours later the FBI picked up a man exiting the very same I-25 freeway and slung him in jail after discovering he was carrying another extortion note he'd written to a wealthy banker in Hendersonville. It later emerged that the black limo following June's daughters was actually a movie scout who wanted them both to appear in a film.

That blackmail scare was a cold reminder to Johnny Cash that there were definite disadvantages to fame that could never be overcome. From then on, he had a bodyguard in the house at all times and also employed a minder to 'clear' the property before he and his family arrived following a trip away, or even a dinner engagement for that matter.

Johnny and June got another jolt when the whole family plus friends Kris Kristofferson and Shel Silverstein flew off to New York City to perform at Madison Square Garden. On arrival at JFK, the captain informed them that a death threat had been made against Johnny and they were to leave the plane immediately. The source of the threat was never uncovered.

Johnny went ahead with his concert that night, but his steely eyes snapped around the auditorium filled with twenty thousand fans, wondering if the stalker was out there. June was so freaked out by these threats that she started carrying a Swiss army knife around in her handbag. She would not go anywhere without it, even after accidentally opening it one night and inflicting a wound in the palm of her own hand that required seven stitches.

By 1974, Johnny was leading a totally drug-free life and proud to tell anyone who wanted to listen about the mistakes he'd made in the past. The most remarkable aspect of Johnny's openness was that he was probably the first superstar to actually hold his hands up and admit what he'd done in the past. Within ten years dozens of celebrities would have done likewise, but most of them freely admitted Johnny Cash was their inspiration. He was the guy who had the courage to stand up and say he'd been there first. Yet only a couple of years earlier everyone had written Johnny Cash off. They had seen the singer as someone who'd had his day and should retire quietly and gracefully from the music scene. But Cash had no intention of doing that.

The 'new' Johnny Cash now injected his religious beliefs into his live shows whenever he could – and the audiences lapped it up. While in previous years his fans had simply interpreted his songs as coming directly from the demons he'd dealt with, now Cash was wearing a halo around his head and the same songs were being interpreted in an entirely different way.

Johnny was perceived as a man who was wiser, older and regretful of his previous years of wasted life at the hands of the demon drink and drugs. His family frequently joined him on stage for his final number, including his daughter Rosanne and June's child Carlene, as well as June herself.

The year 1976 marked an extraordinary resurgence in country music. Johnny Cash was now being seen in a contemporary vein, the meanings of his songs reinterpreted to fit the uprising of the 'urban cowboy', a sissified version of the hero of the Old West, and country & western dance clubs were filled each night with businessmen and women learning 'the Texas Two-step'.

In early 1976, *Saga Magazine* published a glowing article about the phenomenon of Johnny Cash and his magical voice: 'The Cash bass-baritone resists description and comparison, but it is at its best something like a smooth and mellow thunder. The voice is earthy deep and occasionally ominous, resonant, virile, untrained, and unconventional. It can be lonely, and haunting, coming out as practically a dirge, and the next minute booming happily.'

The magazine also described his performance on 'A Boy Named Sue' as 'More than singing, it is story telling to guitar accompaniment – a bawdy, swinging poem'.

A few months later, *Hustler* magazine published a four-page cartoon strip featuring a shapely and often nude girl singer named Honey Hooker and her visit to Opryland. Cash and several other singers, including Dolly Parton, Charley Pride, Mel Tillis and Loretta Lynn were portrayed in easily identifiable caricatures, performing various lewd sexual acts and were given fictitious, soundalike names, all of which had definite sexual connotations. Cash was not amused. His attorney made a statement to the press saying, 'For the record, Johnny Cash is incensed over the whole thing. We are considering taking legal action, but no judgement has been made at this time.' Charley Pride was just as furious: 'It's a concoction by sick people out to make a dollar. I think it's horrible and I don't appreciate it.'

In early 1977, Johnny went on a strict diet, shed more than 35 pounds and announced to his fans that he was increasing the number of live appearances he would perform. After Johnny's earlier battles with pills, he found he had sunk into near obesity. He was miserable, uncomfortable and had become lazy and disinterested in his musical career. Losing weight gave him a new energy for life. Naturally, he gave credit to June and insisted he'd discovered new foods, 'like grains and things', that made him feel much healthier.

Johnny saw his new energy as yet more evidence of his love for June. She had helped him kick the pills and revitalise his career and now she was helping him through another, smaller crisis. Cash saw his marriage to June as lasting because of the daily acts of charity they showed to one another. He later explained: 'It's goin' the second mile and bendin' over. Turnin' the other cheek. We share an old-fashioned Christian faith.'

Despite Cash's glowing tribute to his wife, reports eventually surfaced that suggested the singer was having an affair and was back on drugs. *The National Enquirer* ran a story which stated that 'Johnny Cash is brawling mad over rumours sweeping Nashville that he's back on drugs and that his wife recently caught him romancing her close friend.' The story was one of those classic no-smoke-without-fire articles that had Johnny denying everything, which simply gave the magazine a chance to publish all their allegations, including the claims that Cash, to spite his wife, fired his back-up vocal group, the Carter Sisters; that Cash was high on drugs when he taped his latest television special, *Johnny and Friends*; and that he was forced to cancel planned appearances in two Billy Graham crusades because of boozing.

The rumours about Johnny and Jan romancing were particularly detailed and included a claim that she had become pregnant by the singer and had been forced to go into hospital to have an abortion. A furious Johnny later insisted that the story was rubbish. He denied all the claims emphatically, telling the *Enquirer*, 'If I weren't a Christian, I'd break the jaws of three or four people around this town who are putting these stories around.'

Even as Cash made several public statements denying the rumours, the stories of his extra-marital activities continued to circulate, especially in Nashville. Johnny insisted to one reporter, 'June and I are too much in love to ever separate,' adding that rumours about him firing members of his group were due to a 'reorganisation' of his road show. As for the drugs, Cash insisted, 'I swear that I have never used heroin or sniffed cocaine. And I am not on pills, and I haven't been since several years ago.'

It seemed as if Johnny would never be able to entirely shake off the demons that stalked him. By confessing his sins to the world he'd actually opened yet another can of worms. As he said at the time, 'I'm just glad these people spreading the rumours are talking about me – and not about them – because I would be the one that would have to pay in the end for telling lies.'

Even after issuing numerous lengthy denials, Johnny continued to be haunted by those rumours of an affair. Within the Nashville music industry, the stories were actually gaining strength and they now included claims that Johnny was back on pills as well. Johnny continued to insist his only preoccupation at that time was reorganising his roadshow. He insisted the new-look roadshow had been brought about for financial *not* romantic reasons.

Johnny also announced to the world that, while June and he had been vacationing in the Caribbean, they once again exchanged their wedding vows with son John Carter Cash acting as best man. 'It just happened spontaneously. June said out of the blue, "Why don't we get married again?" And I said, "Why not?" I love her more than ever.'

The stories of Johnny's alleged affair finally ran out of steam. In the middle of all this, Johnny and June managed to put together a musical movie on Jesus called *Gospel Road* which Johnny bravely described as 'a movie designed to be entertaining, carrying the identification mark of my music, but a movie that is an expression of our faith; our witness and testimony and the overshadowing power in it to be the words of Jesus'.

At least one national TV sponsor voiced an interest in the movie, but insisted that the project would have to get network script approval. Johnny would have none of that. He told one bemused TV executive, 'This film is gonna be an extension of ourselves – an expression of our faith, told however we feel it when the cameras start to roll.' TV companies soon lost interest.

For thirty long days, Johnny, June and their cast and crew

toiled away in Israel to produce this dream project. It was an exhausting month and there were definitely moments when Johnny wondered if it had all been a dreadful mistake. One day he admitted to June: 'What a mountain we have chosen to climb this time. Where did we ever get the idea we knew anythin' about producin' a movie?'

But June had the perfect answer, 'Let's don't call it a movie. Let's call it our "testimony". We know how to do that.'

Johnny and June eventually returned home to Nashville with their mission accomplished. But then the really tough job of editing the film had to start. Nine more arduous months were spent cutting and recutting, writing songs, recording them and then carefully adding them to the film. It was much harder than any of them had at first realised. Just before the release of *Gospel Road*, Kris Kristofferson visited June and Johnny in their hotel room in New York and sang them two songs he'd just written. They decided on the spot to make sure that one of his songs, 'Burden of Freedom', was used in the movie.

Gospel Road was picked up for distribution by 20th Century-Fox, but after a year of indecision on how to market the movie Billy Graham's World Wide Pictures took it over and eventually it was shown to packed churches all over the US. A print of the movie was also taken and shown to more than 150,000 prisoners from New York to California and hundreds of those prisoners wrote personally to Johnny to thank him for making the film.

By the US's Labor Day holiday of 1974, Johnny Cash was feeling almost as stressed and overworked as he had before he'd kicked drink and drugs all those years earlier. Every day and every hour of his life seemed to be taken up by work, concerts, recordings, TV specials, appearances for this or that cause, day after day, week after week. Johnny Cask knew he was being spread a little too thin.

By this time he'd purchased a farm at Bon Aqua, an hour west of Nashville and in the middle of 1974, he headed up there with June for a few days' rest. But on arrival at the farm Cash got a call that nearly brought his world crashing down all around him; their son John Carter and several of his friends were in hospital after a car crash. The youngsters had been rescued from the wreckage of Johnny's sister Reba's jeep by a group of the singer's fans who were gawping at the house in Hendersonville at the time of the crash.

Initially, Cash didn't know what had happened to his son. At the hospital, Johnny's neighbour and friend Roy Orbison and his wife Barbara provided a shoulder to cry on. Orbison's first wife had died in a motorcycle accident and two of his own children died in a fire in the house next to Johnny's just a few months afterwards. Many years later, June remembered the accident in deadly serious terms and still referred to their son John Carter being given a 'fifty-fifty chance to live'. She and Johnny also never forgot the care and attention given to them by Roy Orbison. Fortunately, the accident turned out not to be as serious as at first feared, although it reminded Johnny of how important his family were to him. The couple's children played an increasingly important role in Cash's life, and he felt he was at last proving himself to be a good father to them all.

Daughter Rosanne graduated from high school in Ventura in 1973 and then moved in with her father and stepmother in

Hendersonville, working with the couple in concert. Kathleen, eighteen at the time, also moved to Tennessee from California and joined the staff of the House of Cash. Stepdaughter Carlene performed regularly with June and Johnny until her marriage to singer-writer Jack Ruth, who'd just signed a recording contract with RCA Victor.

For the first time in his adult life, Johnny was at the centre of a happy, family unit and he couldn't quite believe it had all happened.

15

FAMILY IN PERIL

It was 1977. Johnny Cash heard an explosive crash of fresh air rushing through that big house in Hendersonville. It was a cruel and hard noise, not the gentle whistle of the wind they were used to. Suddenly, young John Carter woke in his bed and started crying. June, aware that something bad was happening outside, scooped the child out of his bed and rocked him back and forth against her breast. Then June called out for Carlene, Rosey and their cousin Suzie, just as they entered the front door downstairs after a night out in nearby Nashville.

'Get behind the big fireplace. Quick!'

The whirlwind outside was picking up objects and hurling them against the side of the house. June leaped out of the bedroom with Johnny Cash alongside her and they both ran down the stairs. Suddenly there was a huge explosion and the house seemed to shake on its foundations. The Cashes and Carters flung themselves to the floor and waited to die.

Then the windows and doors flew open. This was followed by dust and water pouring through the house. More exploding noises rattled under the property. The air was so thick with debris that neither Johnny nor June could see what was happening outside. It looked and felt as though a huge black funnel was whirling through the property. In fact, Johnny Cash and his family had just survived a tornado.

Moments later, June glanced out of the window and noticed their neighbour Braxton Dixon's house had disappeared. Johnny went out to investigate and discovered that the other house had been completely flattened and bits of it had landed on the Cash roof, giving rise to the explosive noises they'd heard earlier. Johnny's extraordinary knack of surviving anything God or others could fling at him had won through yet again.

A few months later he found himself at the centre of a different kind of near miss when he took a call from the legendary Sam Phillips to say that Elvis Presley was dead. Cash was stunned by the news, if not that surprised. It could so easily have been him, although he'd held on to the two things Elvis did not manage to retain – his family and his independence. The two megastars hadn't met in more than ten years, though they'd closely monitored each other's career throughout that time. But while Johnny Cash had finally turned the corner and started to mend fences and cure his addictions, Elvis had dipped deeper and deeper into an abyss of pill-popping and teams of sycophants. He'd lost touch with reality long before he died.

Later Johnny speculated on why they'd never met during those last few tragic years of Elvis's life. He even wondered if it was predestined that they'd go their separate ways. Johnny knew Elvis had been a waste towards the end – and he kept casting his mind back to his own bad old times. Elvis's death was a lesson he should never forget, something to help him make sure he didn't slip off the rails ever again.

By the late 1970s, it was becoming clear that Johnny Cash had the sort of staying power none of his detractors from the bad old days could have predicted. Although renowned for his 'hillbilly' music, Johnny Cash had more than proved himself no hick. Few of his fans realised that the man who'd seemed to have so much in common with the prisoners he sang to had actually developed expensive tastes when it came to hotel accommodation as he criss-crossed the US. It was all a far cry from the early days on the road. Now Cash's tours were extremely well planned and featured sumptuous hotel suites booked months in advance, places where 'French provincial' and 'Danish modern' were the bywords for real style.

When Johnny and June were booked into the Marriott, in Woodland Hills, California, they discovered the couple who'd booked the wedding suite ahead of them had been bumped down to make way for the celebrity couple. Immediately they walked into the wedding reception with their suitcases still in their hands, having just arrived on the tour bus. The band started playing 'I Married You in Jackson' and then Cash sang another one of his hits, 'The Ways of a Woman in Love'. Johnny and June stayed for more than half an hour at the reception of bride Angela Scaglione and her groom Glenn Hoerner, who later recalled:

'It was great to have him here. He and June put the icing on the cake.'

But, as Johnny's career moved further and further away from those far-off days when he and the Tennessee Three endlessly toured the nation, the group itself began to crumble. Bass player Marshall Grant left the group in March 1980 – acrimoniously – although the matter was kept very quiet at the time. Perhaps not surprisingly, Grant filed a legal suit against Johnny, six months later asking for an audit of Cash's records, as well as $3.9 million in compensatory and punitive damages for alleged slanderous statements that Cash made about Grant plus breach of contract. Grant alleged that Cash had dissolved their partnership in a letter in March 1980. Grant, by now living in Hernando, Mississippi, contended that he never actually received his share of the proceeds from the partnership. The lawsuit also alleged that through the years Grant and the late lamented Luther Perkins had asked for their share of the money, but each time, according to the suit, Cash 'would become angry and at times violent when questioned about these monies, maintaining he would take care of the matter'. It was also claimed that 'because of the defendant's [Cash's] violent tendencies and out of fear of triggering further anger and violence, the two finally ceased to press the matter'. Grant, who was earning $100,000 a year with Cash, claimed he was promised an annual salary of that amount for the rest of his life, or until he could no longer perform. He was asking for $1.3 million to compensate for lost wages.

By 1981, Johnny Cash's wise investing of his estimated $40 million fortune meant he was now comfortable enough to purchase a winter estate in Montego Bay, Jamaica. The house was set on a former sugar plantation, and Cash kept a year-round housekeeper called Edith Montague on the premises. But that Christmas an incident was to occur that provided Cash and his family with yet another brush with death. The entire family, including June, Johnny's sister Reba, her husband Chuck Hussey, eleven-year-old John Carter Cash, a friend, Johnny and beloved housekeeper Edith, found themselves the victims of a violent robbery at their house in Jamaica. They were in the midst of a pre-meal prayer when three stocking-clad men burst through the double doors of the dining room.

'What do you want?' demanded Johnny, springing to his feet.

The robbers – all of Jamaican descent – replied simply, 'Everytin'.'

Johnny was emphatic, 'You can have all our money. You can have anything you want. Don't hurt the children. Don't do something you'll be sorry for.'

Just then one of them grabbed little John Carter by the hair, pulling him up off the floor by his father. June could not breathe with fear. She looked across at Johnny Cash.

Just then the one with the gun screamed, 'Search them all.'

'We're hungry.'

'We want your money.'

'I'll shoot you.'

Then one of them shoved his gun in John Carter's ear. There were gasps from the victims. John Carter said nothing.

June later gave this dramatic account of what happened: 'I'm scared to death. My face is on the floor. My husband might kill somebody. We might try to help him. John Carter's just staring straight ahead. Old Sharp Knife [one of the robbers] is crawling over bodies on the floor, nearer and nearer to me. I'm having a hard time breathing. How could they? How dare they?'

The robbers then searched every room in the house, holding guns to the heads of Johnny and all the rest in turn as they took one prisoner up to the rooms to hunt for valuables. At one stage, June was dragged by her long, flowing chestnut hair to a bedroom. It looked really ominous to the others and the robber kept mentioning how nice her hair was. Once in the bedroom the man ripped the mattress off the bed as he searched for money and jewellery. But June remained untouched.

Back downstairs, their son John Carter seemed the only victim who was unafraid. At one point the leader of the robbers yelled out: 'Somebody's gonna die here tonight if we don't get what we want.' Then, as an afterthought he added, 'I like you, little redheaded boy.'

John Carter replied, 'Thank you, sir.'

The criminals eventually got what they wanted – including $50,000 worth of cash and jewellery – plus 175 pairs of shoes that were due to go to a local charity. Then they forced the family to lie face down on the floor, swearing and shouting at the entire party in the process. Some of the victims were convinced they were about to die.

'Do not look up! Keep your face down on the floor. All of you – down.'

The gang then changed their mind and forced Cash and his family all down to the wine cellar in the basement and locked them inside it. Johnny and his brother-in-law were able to break through the wall, freeing guests within 45 minutes. It emerged that the bandits had actually lifted the entire meal from the dinner table and taken it with them when they fled in one of the Cashes' Land Rovers. The entire house was trashed.

Minutes after the robbers left, Cash jumped in his own Land Rover and drove three miles to a police station to report the robbery. A few hours later, a resident of Barreltown spotted the stolen Land Rover nine miles from the Cash mansion. As the robbers were removing their 'booty' from the vehicle, a nearby resident recognised the car, grabbed a machete and chased the men, who fled into the nearby Jamaican mountains.

Due to the incident, the Cash family cut short their vacation and immediately returned home to Nashville. But the bad memories of Jamaica were soon put in perspective when, under very tragic circumstances, two friends were shot and killed during a robbery just two miles from the house near Hendersonville. It seemed as if nowhere was truly safe any more.

Jamaican Prime Minister Edward P Seaga personally apologised to Johnny for the robbery and spoke several times to him following his return to Tennessee. June Carter was severely shaken by the incident. As she later recalled: 'I've never in my life been more truly frightened. Being scared didn't surprise me, being angry did. For I was angry at these men who came into my house, threatened those I loved most and wanted to steal or break things that were rightfully mine. The fear faded, but the anger is still there.'

Johnny was told shortly after his arrival back in Tennessee in June, 1981, that he would be on the receiving end of yet another lawsuit. This time Linda Revious of Colorado Springs – the daughter of deceased Johnny Cash band member Luther Perkins – had filed a lawsuit charging that Johnny owed her late father hundreds of thousands of dollars in royalties. The suit also named Marshall Grant as a responsible party. Revious's two sisters were co-plaintiffs.

'We're not asking the court to give us anything that we're not entitled to,' explained Revious. 'Johnny Cash is a legend because of Perkins and Grant. He didn't do it all by himself. It was the three of them that really created the songs that Cash is famous for.'

The lawsuit demanded that the court determine the amount of money that Cash and Grant owed Perkins's estate in royalties from the sale of recordings, income from the sale of books, programmes and souvenirs, compensation for performances and other money that the plaintiffs alleged that their father did not receive. Not surprisingly, the publicity fallout from such allegations wasn't good for Johnny. It tainted the 'good ole country boy' image so carefully nurtured by his management. Now the so-called man of the people seemed more of a greedy celebrity. Eventually, both suits with Revious and Marshall Grant were settled out of court.

In 1981, the Country Music Hall of Fame finally recognised Johnny Cash and inducted him with a lavish ceremony attended by many other legends of country music – and, of course, his family. Cash's daughters were already beating a path through the country music business. Rosanne, now 25, was enjoying fame as a country singer and songwriter, while married to another prominent songwriter, Rodney Crowell. Carlene Carter had divorced, remarried producer, songwriter and rock musician Nick Lowe and now had two daughters. Kathy Cash, 24, was in charge of the complex network of Cash song-publishing companies while Cindy Cash, 22, was singing with her father on the road. Tara Cash, 19, was an up-and-coming actress.

Life seemed to be once more looking up for Johnny Cash. Besides the house near Nashville and that mansion in Jamaica, there was another home in Florida, a rural Tennessee farm, an apartment in New York, and several other houses lodging relatives and friends. The man who'd grown up on beans now had a son with a taste for caviar. The value of what Johnny actually owned was scarcely calculable. As far as he was concerned, he never needed to know.

But Johnny remained obsessed with the longevity of his career. Ever since his red-hot popularity in the late 1960s – which many reckoned peaked on TV in those prime-time series – he'd struggled to recapture momentum. Johnny himself genuinely feared that his Hall of Fame election was simply his swan song.

He was still commanding at least $30,000 a night on the concert trail and his endless series of spots for an Amoco television commercial earned him more than $1 million – even though it also earned him flak from energy preservationists, since the commercials were being broadcast at the height of America's first serious fuel crisis. Johnny had just released his LP *Rockabilly Blues*, on which he attempted a return to the root sound that first made him famous. At concerts to promote the album, he'd stay on stage for almost two hours. Instead of a tired and pat recital of the obligatory hits, his performance was an ambitious, fast-moving and exciting mixture of past and present.

But, beneath the energetic exterior, Johnny Cash still remained in personal turmoil. There wasn't a day that went by when he didn't think about pills. He still had to be incredibly careful because taking just one tablet could spark off all those old problems. The fight was from within but it was still raging. Cash took great pride in his ability to resist the 'demon drugs', although there were definitely times when he was feeling so low that he desperately felt the need for something to lift him. That's when he craved it, but he couldn't have it and that simply made him want it even more.

Johnny wasn't doing so well on the recording front, either. While Hendersonville neighbour Roy Orbison's fortunes had revived – he now seemed to be on a par with Chuck Berry and Duane Eddy according to a *Record Collector* popularity poll – Johnny was way below that line-up, alongside Del Shannon and Carl Perkins. That grated with him. He wanted to be number one all the time.

His fortunes were improved somewhat when Roy Orbison, Carl Perkins, Jerry Lee Lewis and Cash recorded an album together at the newly modernised Sun Studio, back in Memphis. The idea had been born four years earlier when Sun issued a jam session from 1956 allegedly involving the 'Million Dollar Quartet' of Lewis, Cash, Perkins and Elvis. More of documentary interest than anything else, this thirty-minute singsong nonetheless provoked sufficient response for a premeditated Eighties reconstruction of the 'Class of 55' – with Roy Orbison filling in for the now deceased Elvis.

For Johnny it was a matter of swallowing his pride and getting on with a golden opportunity. He wasn't exactly the best of buddies with Jerry Lee Lewis since that flare-up when the two were making a Christmas Special together back in the Seventies. But that was now all water under the bridge. They had a job to do.

The resulting album was called *Homecoming*, a likeable enough sentimental journey, rife with tuneful reminiscences, slices of autobiography in song plus a commemoration of Elvis. But music industry observers quickly pointed out that Johnny and Roy Orbison were the least active of the chicken-necked principals, submitting only one solo turn each against the others' two. The remaining four tracks were communal efforts, with verses doled out more or less equally and everyone in raucous harmony on the choruses.

Around this time, Johnny was urged by an old friend, former president Jimmy Carter, to try and use a word processor for his writing. Purist Johnny preferred yellow legal pads and a pen and usually claimed he wrote best on buses and in hotel rooms – although he did gradually come round to the idea of working in the log cabin he owned in the grounds of that vast Tennessee mansion next to Old Hickory Lake.

Walking through the groves of the hickory trees one day in 1982, mulling over the contents of a novel he was planning to write, Cash ran into the ostrich that lived in the wildlife preserve he'd recently set up in the grounds of the house. Fearing the bird was hostile, Johnny waved a stick at it. In response, the ostrich started to charge. Cash bellowed something at it and the creature darted away. A few minutes later the two met again, and this time the ostrich leaped into the air and slammed its taloned feet against Johnny's chest. It then began clawing Johnny and was stopped only by his heavy metal belt buckle. Johnny Cash ended up with five broken ribs.

There seemed no end to the disasters that plagued the man's life.

16

FACING UP TO
RESPONSIBILITIES

The boy and his father crouched by the river bank having built a fine fire and were singing a stream of songs old and new. This was Johnny Cash's idea of a dream come true. Here he was in the middle of the Tennessee countryside with his only son for company, plus their faithful coon dog, known to all and sundry as Mollie Carter Cash. Johnny had waited many years to have a son to truly bond with, but it was worth it in the end because by all accounts he forged a very close relationship with John Carter, despite the fact Cash was an elderly daddy by anyone's standards.

Some nights, the two would sit out and talk for hours about all the things Johnny used to speak of with his late, much-lamented brother Jack. In the distance, coon dogs would howl and yell as they chased the long-tailed animals who inhabited so much of Hickman County, Tennessee. The dogs would only stop once the coons had climbed up the tallest trees to escape the hounds.

Often, Cash and his beloved son would stand up and pee on their campside fire while singing coon-rallying songs, in the finest tradition of the county. Then Johnny would get up and shake the tree where that coon was hiding until it fell out of the sky. Other times he'd leave it to its own devices. 'It all depended on what kinda mood I was in,' Cash later explained.

With these new-found priorities, Johnny Cash planned his life with much more care and responsibility. One time he explained to June that he wanted to take her and their son somewhere no one had ever been. Time was flying by. Soon their son would be gone. He'd have a girlfriend, and they'd only have memories of his childhood to keep them happy in their old age.

But then June and Johnny Cash should have known better. The couple had been involved in so many near-death experiences that it was becoming a running joke, even among their millions of fans. TV chat show host Johnny Carson used to crack jokes about Johnny's health on a regular basis. It was always of matter of not *if* something would happen but *when*.

This time Johnny Cash wanted to take his wife and son to ride the rapids in the Alaskan wilderness. So the family flew off to Anchorage, Alaska, and took another jet the next day to the port of Dillingham where they were met by a seaplane that would deposit them at the Tikchik Narrow Lodge. 'And that's where our adventure will begin,' promised Johnny. From the lodge they flew in a single-engine plane across the Tikchik Narrows River and over treetops, buzzing caribou, bear and moose before boarding two small boats to ride the rapids.

Within a day, John Carter had almost drowned in the river's swirling currents and June found herself wishing she was back in the comfort of Nashville. Johnny joked his way through, even when both boats were swept away. The last two days of the vacation were spent huddled under a tree hoping that an aircraft would spot them and organise a rescue party. Eventually all three got back to Nashville in one piece, but Johnny decided from then on to stick to more traditional vacations.

Not long after his return home, Johnny Cash took another, much more nostalgic trip back to his childhood home in Dyess, Arkansas. Within seconds of entering the one-time family house, Johnny found himself walking gently across the creaking wooden floor, still afraid to make too much noise in case he woke the other children.

'Reba. Reba,' he called to his sister, who'd made the nostalgic journey with him. 'Take a look.'

Johnny pointed down at the holes in the floor of the kitchen as the memories came flooding back for both of them. The holes in the floor had been caused by burning chunks of wood that had fallen out of the stove on to the floor when their mother used the stove throughout the Thirties and the Forties. Johnny could vividly remember how he and his brothers and sisters would cut the wood up and pile it next to the stove – 'laying-by time'.

Suddenly, Johnny Cash felt a shiver run right through his body; he remembered how, at the age of four, he'd fallen into the stove and burned his hand. He had been lucky that he wasn't seriously injured. But he could still remember every single scream of pain.

Cottonwood trees still surrounded the house. Johnny had never forgotten how his father pulled them up from the riverbank and brought them up to the house to shade the property. He remembered exactly what he was doing at certain moments. Every room, every window, every wall had a memory. He stood there in the house, on a voyage back to his past, close to tears.

• • • •

Ask any great man and he'll tell you that even the best of intentions do not necessarily guarantee success. And such was the case with Johnny Cash. He believed in his heart he was born to be a great man, somebody who'd be a true achiever. But he loved the Lord and held his faith above everything else in his life. He also recognised that he was a mere man and men were the pawns of temptation.

In March, 1983, Johnny – who'd suffered numerous illnesses over the years – was admitted to the Baptist Hospital, in Tennessee, with pneumonia. By a strange twist of fate his wife June was also admitted to the same hospital at exactly the same time to undergo an operation to correct a complication caused by abdominal surgery performed earlier that year.

Rumours about Cash's ill health had long been circulating the Nashville country circuit after the Man in Black became sick during a tour in late 1982. One piece of ludicrous gossip suggested Cash was suffering from AIDs, a disease that had only recently become known to the public at large. In February, 1983, Cash developed a serious sinus infection and laryngitis, but continued to perform in defiance of doctors' advice. One of the driving forces behind Cash's determination not to bow out of his commitments was the promise he gave his manager Lou Robin to go back and perform at auditoriums where he'd failed to show up during the bad old days.

In the ultimate irony, Cash's illnesses had actually been brought on by his years of drug abuse and addiction. And the drugs being used to treat his illnesses at this time had a tragic side-effect on the singer's body – his old physical weaknesses started to reawaken. It had happened once before, in South-East Asia. Now he was in real danger of suffering another relapse. Soon Cash was popping dozens of pills every day and, worse still, he thought that June and the rest of his family had not even noticed.

This time around, June grew even more distraught because she thought she'd got him off drugs years earlier. But this was even worse: she didn't even feel she could throw his bottles of pills away whenever she found them. She decided her self-abusing husband had to take the responsibility himself. He was going to have to deal with the devil's work all alone.

It was only during a whistle-stop tour of Europe in the spring of 1983 that June told her husband: 'I believe you have a problem.'

'What're you talkin' about? I don't have a problem.'

'Well, good for you,' came June's cold reply. 'Because I think I have a problem now myself, emotionally, and I can't handle what you're doin'.'

Johnny walked away without uttering another word. June was heartbroken because she had wanted to help him although she felt on this occasion she had to detach herself because she couldn't handle the situation. To let go was the hardest thing in the world to do, but she believed it would help him in the long run.

June then took the hardest decision of her life and walked out on her husband until he decided to clean himself up. She moved to England where her daughter Carlene lived and let Cash travel back to Nashville alone. She busied herself at Carlene's home by keeping her daughter's house immaculately tidy and playing with her grandchildren. The world never even knew that Johnny and June had split up. It was one of the best-kept secrets in showbusiness.

Cash was distraught at the split and ordered his management to keep it quiet in the hope that June would come back before anyone found out what had happened. Meanwhile, he seriously doubted whether he could live without her. He tried to call June, but she wanted space and refused to respond to his approaches. June later said she felt she'd reached a crossroads in her life and was not sure which way to turn.

June was still in England in the late autumn of 1983 when Cash suffered severe back spasms, which prompted his doctor to put him on even more medication. This was followed by a serious bout of blood poisoning caused by an insect bite. Then, on November 22, 1983, Cash underwent surgery for a bleeding ulcer during which portions of his stomach had to be removed. There seemed to be no end to Johnny Cash's health problems.

When June heard about the ulcer, she hopped on a Concorde in London and flew back to be at her husband's bedside. But the moment he began to recover her old fears returned. With each new illness, doctors were introducing yet another type of drug into Cash's bloodstream. After the last piece of surgery, they put him on morphine for ten days and his body rapidly became totally dependent on it.

One day, June, teenage son John Carter and Dr Joe Cruse, a physician from the Betty Ford Center for drug and alcohol treatment, gathered around Johnny's bed at the Baptist Hospital, in Nashville, and pleaded with him to enter the Ford Center. At first, Cash was extremely reluctant. He believed the news would leak out and his fans would be disappointed in him. It was an admission of guilt that he just couldn't come to terms with.

Then Dr Cruse informed Cash he'd probably die within the next few months unless he took some drastic action. Johnny looked across at June and their son John Carter and weakly nodded his head in agreement. In mid-December, 1983, a statement was issued to the press by Johnny's worried management. It stated that Johnny was voluntarily entering the Betty Ford Center, located in The Eisenhower Medical Center, in Rancho Mirage, California, in order to 'avoid dependency on painkillers he had taken during a recent illness'.

The world of showbusiness was rocked by the news. Everyone knew about Johnny's previous battles with booze and drugs, but he'd cheerily announced to the world he'd beaten those demons years earlier. To his fans, Cash had been clean and sober for a long time. Many started to wonder whether he'd ever been on the straight and narrow in the first place. There was talk of a long-standing cover-up by his management. It was a public relations disaster for Johnny Cash.

The stark truth was that Cash couldn't cope with the introduction of any chemical into his bloodstream. Even an aspirin had the potential to turn into an addictive substance for someone with the weaknesses of the Man in Black. Many people found this hard to believe, but his family knew the truth. They'd been with him on so many occasions when he'd won his battle against the demons. But they knew all along that Johnny would probably never win the actual war.

Cash told well-known TV reporter Barbara Walters during a rare onscreen interview, 'A man who is strong emotionally and physically, a lot is expected of him. And I felt at times there was too much expected of me. I guess I wanted a security blanket. I wanted to hide from that.' What Johnny did not tell Barbara Walters was that he was convinced the demons would never completely depart. It was easy talking about his past addictions, but facing up to his current problems was a much harder task. Johnny also felt no confidence about his current career; he felt he might be a singer who'd had his day. Trouble was, he hadn't faded from the limelight, so speaking of his past problems simply wasn't enough for his adoring public. They wanted the whole truth. The rumour machine was working overtime trying to put Cash down, to destroy him, because no one really knew precisely what was happening.

Inside the Betty Ford Center, Johnny stuck to a strict daily regime and later described his stay there as 'the best six weeks of my life. I learned a lot about drugs and a lot about myself.' He also was eternally grateful to the ever dependable Dr Cruse. Before entering the clinic, Johnny had been experiencing terrible pain and hallucinations. The nightmares had got so bad he'd left his bed, only to be found wandering around the hospital where he was staying. He later admitted he'd been seriously considering taking his own life. The pain and anguish had seemed too much to bear. He knew he'd ruined other people's lives and perhaps it was time to end his own to stop all those others suffering.

But, inside the Betty Ford Center, Johnny Cash learned a lot more about himself and the disease that was threatening his life. He was taught what chemical dependency really meant and how he could cope with it. For those six long weeks, Johnny rose at 6:30am, had breakfast at 7:00am and began an imposing round of daily activities, including lectures and group therapy sessions in which, he later explained, 'about ten people in a group got into each other's heads, tried to understand each other's problems and worked at working them out.'

Johnny's old friend Kris Kristofferson brought him a book about the bank-robbing brothers Jesse and Frank James and the two stars decided they'd try and make a movie together about the two criminals. NBC's *The Last Days of Frank and Jesse James*, which starred both Johnny and June, attracted extremely high ratings when it was finally broadcast; television networks were at last waking up to the fact that country stars attracted big audiences.

During the fourth week of treatment, June and John Carter joined the singer inside the centre for one of the family programme sessions. On Cash's departure from the centre, he set aside five weeks just to be with his family. He wanted to celebrate his sixteenth wedding anniversary with June as well as being there in person for John Carter's fourteenth birthday. Cash also immediately got himself involved in helping finance a $6.5 million retirement centre in Madison as a memorial to June's mother, Maybelle, who'd died back in October, 1978.

And, throughout all this pain and anguish, Johnny Cash's popularity continued undiminished. Just months after his release from the Betty Ford Center, he starred in a well-received made-for-TV movie called *Murder In Coweta County* with wife June. He also continued to sell out venues across the United States and abroad.

By early 1984, Johnny once again began being publicly open about his problems. He told the *Nashville Banner*, 'Drugs are something that you can get addicted to and hooked on. Everybody's fallible and everybody's vulnerable.' He even admitted in that interview that he'd been treated with morphine for his bleeding ulcer and added, 'With that and the other medication that I was taking, I was well on the road to becoming a confirmed addict, a terminal addict.'

Later in 1984, Johnny and June planned a very special tour to Russia to perform in two cities, Leningrad and Moscow. The couple were excited about the trip because it was the first time either of them had ever been in the communist bloc. Johnny Cash had strange memories of those far-off days in the Air Force in the early Fifties when it was his job to track Russian military movements. He'd always been curious about what *they* – the enemy – were really like. The trip was eventually scheduled for September and, as a last-minute precaution, June decided to go for a health check-up with her long-standing and very trusted doctor in Nashville, John Truppin. Truppin had become a close friend of the Cashes and had been June's gynaecologist during her pregnancy with John Carter. As June would say to Johnny and her family, 'He had an even better view of me than other men, except John.' But when she called the doctor's office to make an appointment she was stunned to discover that her friend and confidant had been on board the ill-fated Korean Airlines Flight 007, which was shot down by the Russians when it strayed into their airspace. June and Johnny were so stunned by the news that they cancelled the trip to the Soviet Union.

Their trepidation about airplane journeys would prove well founded.

17

FIGHTING BACK

June Carter's nose was virtually stuck to the porthole window on the DC9 airliner she, Johnny Cash and the rest of the 'Johnny Cash Show' troupe were flying on. June later recalled that the fog was so thick she couldn't see the plane's wing as it circled over Lake Erie, Pennsylvania, in preparation for landing. Then she leaned over to Johnny to see if he'd even noticed. He glanced back at her, but didn't utter a word. When she then looked around at her other family and friends on board that day she realised everyone was terrified.

June once again pressed her nose to the window before glancing over at Johnny's sister, Reba. She was smoking furiously and her hair was wet through from sweat. Then June leaned over and held Johnny Cash's hand tightly. She was scared, but thankful that at least they'd decided to leave John Carter back in Nashville.

June then looked across at her sisters, Helen and Anita, and the other band members. She muttered goodbye to them so quietly they never heard her. The plane was lurching from side to side and the passengers braced themselves for the inevitable collision with the fogbound hills that lay just before the airstrip.

As the plane continued its tumble downwards, balking and rearing as the pilot tried to right it, Johnny squeezed June's hand tightly again. Then they both felt the left wing dip down and scrape the ground. A split second later the front end shot up as the pilot fought to control the power of the engines. June glanced out of the porthole and could just about make out the runway, still coming at them at high speed. The plane seemed to be be going much too fast (it was later calculated to have been travelling at more than 200 miles per hour). June later said it felt 'as if we'd been shot from a cannon'.

Just then the nose of the aircraft reared up and the fuselage shook like a rag doll. Everyone, even tough guy Johnny Cash, screamed with terror, and June noticed that the left wing had carved a hole in the ground alongside them. The plane surged upwards once more and limped unsteadily back into the sky through that dense fog. That's when Cash yelled ahead to the pilot through the open cockpit door, 'Can't we just go on to Chicago? Do we have to land here?'

But the plane had already been diverted from Pittsburgh because of bad weather and they were in dire trouble. Their only chance of survival was to land within the next few minutes. Alarm bells were ringing inside in the cockpit. Red lights blinked on and off. Then Johnny, June and all the other passengers heard the mechanical sound of the aircraft's pumps dumping fuel in preparation for a second attempt at landing.

As the aircraft began a new approach towards the airstrip at Lake Erie, Johnny Cash and his entourage put their heads down in their laps and braced themselves. As the aircraft touched the tarmac many of them held their breath. But this time it was a smooth landing without any hiccups, much to everyone's amazement. It was, June later recalled, the most frightening journey of their much-troubled life. For much of the ordeal she'd clasped tightly on to Johnny's huge hand, simply waiting to die.

A ground inspection a few minutes later showed that the DC9's left wing had a piece hanging off it and all the rivets were broken on both wings. The Cashes had yet again somehow lived to see another day.

• • • •

Johnny's problems with drug addiction were well documented. But how June and the rest of the family coped with it all was rarely touched upon, much to the annoyance of Johnny, who felt they'd suffered much worse than he had. June had always remained fairly tight-lipped about the situation. But in her 1987 book *From The Heart* she did explain her true feelings for probably the only time in her life:

> *It's not news to tell you that my husband, John, has a chemical dependency problem. They know it in the good ole U.S.A. They know it in England, Ireland, and*

Scandinavia. They write books on it in Germany – and all the unknown languages seem to get it said without my help. Oh, well here I go again. Let's not talk about him – let's talk about me. A man who drinks, or takes drugs, is having a wonderful time. He is out of his head – his gourd is full – he is flying – his star is in the heavens – for a time. It is the co-dependant that is the sickest. We are the worst of all. We have sunk below the sinkhole – we are in the mire. We are down somewhere in the crevice and the crack. We are in the Ring of Fire and the flames are going higher. We are also very angry. We let go – so we can live. It is very dangerous to let go. I know.

In her book, June recalled how she was deeply touched by a conversation she had with a counsellor at the Betty Ford Center following Johnny's dramatic admittance. Much of the talk had centred around God and Jesus. But at the end of the conversation, June admitted: 'It took me a long time, and John as well, to crawl back up a cliff with no rope – a path with no stepping stones – a way with no will. Yet somewhere – from out of the goodness of God, we made it. I hope you never feel the pain. I would not wish it on anyone.'

Cash's latest 'rebirth' as a cleaned-up act following his cure at the Betty Ford Center definitely marked a change in outlook for the Man in Black. That infamous edge of fury was still definitely there, but another, softer side was emerging. The love of his family had been so paramount to his recovery that he knew he had to show them more love and caring than he had previously managed. And with this new, energised Johnny Cash came a resilience that was to astound many people in the traditionally fickle music industry. Many people genuinely admired Cash for coming out and facing the truth about his addiction problems. Instead of having his fans sniggering behind his back, he'd put his hands up and owned up to everything and they loved him even more for being so honest. That honesty lay at the heart of Johnny Cash's appeal to his fans: he was and always would be a man of his word. To women he was a strong mountain of a man who'd do anything to protect his girl and family and to men he was a tough-guy who took no crap from anyone.

It was that same refusal to take crap from anyone that prompted Johnny to file a lawsuit against Slater-Pichinson Music Inc., charging them with non-payment of money owed from a 1984 song deal. Ironically, this came soon after another lawsuit accusing Johnny of exactly the same behaviour. This latest suit claimed that Slater-Pichinson and its principals had purchased the Cash song catalogue for $1.3 million in 1983 and then failed to pay the last instalment of over $215,000. Cash also claimed the company hadn't paid all royalties due before and after the sale. Like most of the other suits Johnny had been involved with, it was eventually settled out of court.

Of course, fame and fortune inspired a whole host of other problems for the Cashes; the threat of weirdoes and crackpots, for example. Most of the time Johnny and June tried not to let such people get them down, but by the mid-Eighties it seemed as if every live concert appearance they made provoked some kind of death threat.

One time Johnny, June and young John Carter were travelling to New York City from JFK in a rented stretch limo when their vehicle slowed down for some traffic lights. Suddenly, there was an incredible explosion and the rear window of the limo was shattered. All three immediately presumed one of the others had been shot. Millions of tiny slivers of very sharp glass were spread everywhere. Cash looked over anxiously in the direction of his wife and son but all three were unhurt, although June was covered virtually head to toe in glass fragments and did not dare move in case any of them dug into her skin. There was hardly a sliver on either John or John Carter.

Just then, Cash leaned down and grabbed a big round rock from the floor of the limo. He jumped out of the vehicle in a fury. Ahead of him a tall, thin man was scurrying away through the crowded street. By this time, a policeman had joined Johnny in the chase. Back in the limo, June Carter remained in a state of shock, the glass fragments still covering her body. She glanced out of the window to see her husband catch up with the man and wrestle him to the sidewalk. Cash leaned down, rammed the rock in the assailant's face and yelled, 'Is this your rock?' However, the man couldn't speak a word of English and seconds later the policeman took over and arrested him. Johnny, rumpled but unharmed, walked back to the limo and helped June dust off those glass fragments. It was yet another near miss for a man who'd long since got used to courting disaster at every corner. Typically, June later told friends she felt sorry for the man who'd thrown the rock, insisting that he'd been provoked to throw it at them because he'd thought 'we were full-bellied capitalists and represented that symbol of wealth and power'. Johnny laughed off June's theories. As far as he was concerned the man was a sicko who'd almost killed them.

In July, 1986, an article appeared in a Tennessee newspaper claiming that Johnny – who'd been with Columbia Records since 1958 – was about to be dropped by the label. There was little or no explanation as to why this decision had been made. Insiders on Music Row speculated that the reason for the action was that Johnny had not had a solo top ten hit since his 1981 release *The Baron*. Columbia/Epic/CBS head Rick Blackburn's only comment was: 'This is the hardest decision that I've ever had to make in my life.'

Cash was still enjoying a measure of success in duets with Waylon Jennings in their 1986 release 'Even Cowgirls Get The Blues' and he was also a highly valued member of The Highwaymen, the country music supergroup that also comprised Kris Kristofferson, Jennings and Willie Nelson. But his solo records were certainly not selling at the same volume they had a few years previously. In fact, Cash was also signed to two other labels at the same time – PolyGram for his LP compilations, including that reunion album which teamed him with old pals Roy Orbison, Jerry Lee Lewis and Carl Perkins; and Word/Nashville Records for his gospel records. But the news that Columbia were dropping him was shocking to Johnny, who had not been without a proper solo label in over thirty years of recording. Following publication of the article, the reporter who broke the story ran a piece in which he publicly apologised to Columbia chief, Rick Blackburn, stating that he'd taken him out of context and admitting that the story may have caused a problem between Blackburn and Johnny. In reality, the damage between the two men had been long-standing and the relationship would never recover. It seemed strange to many that anyone had bothered extracting an apology from the reporter, since the article proved to be absolutely correct.

A few weeks later, Johnny signed with PolyGram and announced to newsmen: 'I feel great. I'm so happy. This did wonders for my little old ego.' The truth was that Johnny had been completely astounded by Columbia's decision, spent an entire night meditating on his farm and had decided to quit before he was pushed. Cash also informed the press: 'We had a big hug and a few tears and then I walked across the street.'

Johnny's partnership with PolyGram could only mean good things for his career. As a first step, his new label put together a large stack of songs for him to consider recording. It was clear that they were going to be a breath of fresh air compared with his old colleagues at Columbia. PolyGram wanted Cash to join their Mercury Records label and produce a new LP by the first half of the following year. When Johnny dropped in to the PolyGram offices in Nashville, his pal Waylon Jennings showed up to wish him well.

Just two weeks before Johnny's decision to join PolyGram, the label's chief, Steve Popovich, also signed Johnny's old friend Kris Kristofferson. It was all part of the label's massive rebuilding plans in connection with the country music scene.

They'd also recently signed Donna Fargo, Lynn Anderson, Larry Boone, The Wrays and Johnny Paycheck, as well as so-called 'Polka King' Frank Yanokovic.

Immediately after signing with PolyGram, Cash began a promotional tour for the release of his new book, a follow-up to his 1978 autobiography *Man in Black*. The new book was a novel entitled *Man in White*, it outlined the life of the apostle Paul – and it wasn't well received. *Publishers Weekly* proclaimed that 'The author is obviously earnest in his faith, but on the basis of this effort, he is not a novelist.' *The Nashville Banner*, perhaps remaining loyal to one of the city's heroes, insisted that the book 'should stand on its own merit as a well-researched, well-crafted piece of Christian literature'.

Not surprisingly, the book did remarkably well amongst Johnny Cash's more ardent religious fans. Some compared the book's religious doctrine with the life cycle of the singer himself. Cash described the book as being 'about the human and spiritual transformation of a man who thought he was doing right, in the name of God, and was abruptly and immediately shown by God that he was doing it all wrong'. This statement directly reflected Cash's own transformation. He even admitted while promoting his latest book that his drug addiction had gone much deeper and lasted for much longer than had previously been reported.

In January, 1987, grandiose plans were announced for another new direction in the career of Johnny Cash – the Johnny Cash Freedom Train – at a rally in Memphis attended by Johnny and retired General William C Westmoreland, the former commander of United States forces in Vietnam.

Westmoreland had promised that the project – a train ride and travelling show of patriotic music and speeches – would be 'the beginning of a crusade of sorts to rekindle our sense of freedom'. Members of veterans groups from around the country attended that first announcement rally, and veterans in battle fatigues stood honour guard for the programme. Unfortunately, by the following May, a lack of funds from the business community had forced the organisers of the Johnny Cash Freedom Train to cancel a series of patriotic rallies and musical concerts to be held in ten cities, although some shows were still scheduled for Memphis, Pittsburgh and Baltimore. Cash astutely kept a distance from the project once the bad news leaked out. He was bitterly disappointed because he'd genuinely believed there would be great demand for such a patriotic series of events.

Back on the recording front, Johnny worked extremely hard to produce the perfect LP for his new masters at PolyGram, recording 28 songs before picking the ten best that would be used. The title – *Johnny Cash is Coming to Town* – came about because Johnny would have to drive thirty miles from his home in Hendersonville to his producer Jack Clement's place in Nashville. Soon everyone at the studio got to saying, 'Johnny Cash is coming into town today to record', and that line kept hanging in the air. Finally Jack Clement figured that the phrase would make a good album title.

Cash was trying hard to inject his career with some new momentum. He even made a point of performing on stage what people wanted to hear from him, rather than what he felt they wanted. Naturally, he'd introduce new songs at each concert, but he considered the requests from the audience were still his cornerstone. He felt it vital to show them *real* respect. Johnny had never forgotten the words his father told him just after he began making live appearances back in the early 1950s. He'd said: 'You know, son, if the tickets to your show are five dollars, remember each person paid five dollars for the show, and that's how much you're worth that night. Don't let your head swell, because you're only worth five dollars a night. Give 'em their money's worth.'

Johnny Cash also started sitting up and taking notice of some of the newer country artists coming through at the time, such as George Strait, Reba McEntire, Randy Travis, Steve Earle and Dwight Yoakam. They all caught Cash's attention and he strongly approved of what he saw. Then there was his own daughter Rosanne. Johnny Cash positively beamed with pride when he heard her songs and in the spring of 1987, she gave her father a tape of her own recording of 'Tennessee Flat Top Box', which Johnny got a huge kick out of.

Of all the artists at that time, Johnny reckoned that Dwight Yoakam most reminded him of himself twenty or thirty years earlier. He even appreciated the difficulty the young star had initially experienced when he was considered more rockabilly than pure country. Johnny had always considered himself to be a singer prepared to experiment from time to time. After all, he'd been the first country artist to ever use a Tex-Mex trumpet sound – on the recording of 'Ring of Fire' all those years earlier. Dwight Yoakam himself paid the Man in Black the ultimate compliment by recording his own version of 'Ring of Fire', which Johnny rated very highly. Cash also heartily approved of the different factions of country music at the time – especially country rock, which was becoming increasingly popular. He believed that the fans would weed out what they liked best.

In the opening months of 1988, Cash appeared to be enjoying a dramatic new surge in his career. PolyGram planned to release a pair of new Cash albums – a greatest hits compilation entitled *Classic Cash* and an album of duets, *Water From The Wells Of Home*, with such partners as Paul and Linda McCartney, Emmylou Harris, Waylon Jennings, Glen Campbell, Hank Williams Jr, Tom T Hall, Jessi Colter, Roy Acuff, wife June and son John Carter plus daughter Rosanne.

One of the more intriguing cuts on the LP was 'New Moon Over Jamaica', co-written by Johnny, Paul McCartney and Tom Hall and performed by Cash and McCartney with harmonies provided by June, Hall and McCartney's wife Linda. The song marked the first time the ex-Beatle had ever recorded with a country artist. The song was written during an all-night guitar-pulling session at Johnny's vacation mansion on the island of Jamaica. Hall was visiting, and the McCartneys, who were vacationing at their Jamaica home, were invited over to the Cash residence for Christmas dinner. The stars sat up all night on the front porch, singing. Afterwards even Johnny admitted, 'A guitar pull with Paul McCartney is a real trip. He's the only singer I've ever sat with across a porch who plays a guitar left-handed and upside down.'

At about 2:30am with the full moon coming into view, Hall muttered, 'There's a new moon over Jamaica, that's be a good song title.' Cash corrected Hall, pointing out that the moon was full, not new. 'Yeah,' countered Hall, 'but "a new moon" sounds like a better song title.' McCartney and Hall started working on the song together and Cash came in on the chorus and wrote the third verse. Later, McCartney invited Cash to visit his studio in England so that they could record the song together. Cash took a day off from a tour of the UK for the recording. They spent nine hours perfecting it. After the first four hours an impatient Cash suggested doing something else, but McCartney was adamant, stating, 'No, let's get this one right.' Of McCartney, Johnny Cash later said, 'He's not only a joy to work with, he's the ultimate consummate musician. It's got to be just right with him.'

During the late 1980s, Johnny Cash had been hiding appalling pain and depression that sometimes threatened to send him back into the arms of those demon drugs that had haunted his life for so long. He endured a two-year battle with rheumatoid arthritis, but had kept it secret from his family and friends because he didn't want anyone to worry about it. Instead of seeing a doctor, he'd taken aspirin, although that was a risk in itself for a man with such an addictive personality.

Then, in late March, 1988, Cash was struck down with bronchitis and laryngitis just hours after completing a five-night engagement in Las Vegas. He flew straight to California and immediately checked into LA's Eisenhower Memorial Hospital. The singer was suffering from chest pains, fatigue and a nose bleed when he was admitted. Once again, it looked as if Johnny Cash was heading downhill fast.

18

INTO THE NINETIES

For more than thirty years, Johnny Cash had protested that he hated to be bothered, valued his privacy and wanted to be left alone. But it was no secret that he actually craved attention. Part of it was a shrewd realisation that people who get noticed sell more records and receive higher television ratings. There was also his desire to be at the centre of the country music scene. The worst thing you can do to someone like Johnny Cash is to ignore him.

But his admittance to hospital in California after those gruelling Vegas live shows in 1988 made Cash want to crawl under a stone and hope the entire world would forget all about him. Further health problems woke him up to the fact that he'd have to publicly admit those repeated bouts with drugs had caused a huge strain on his health, and that there had been a definite knock-on effect on his marriage and family life.

Wife June Carter had long since returned to the fold after their earlier separation, but he wondered just how much more she could take. 'Alcoholism or drug addiction brings out a lot of character defects in a person. It almost broke up my home and my marriage,' Cash later recalled. 'Thank God for my wife June, a good strong woman who fought the battle with me. It could have led to financial ruin, which it usually does for most people, but, during that period, she had the good sense to be a good business manager.'

This was a remarkable confession by Johnny Cash because he was actually admitting his marriage was close to breaking point. But it was that description of June as a 'good business manager' which had people chuckling. Why on earth should a good wife be expected to play that role as well? Johnny Cash clearly demanded many things from his wife June that others might not have tolerated.

Meanwhile, newspapers and magazines across the US continued to write about Johnny Cash as a 'new person'. This really irritated Cash, because he didn't see himself as some new, cleaned-up version of a former – bad – self. In any case, he was still regularly in and out of hospital, which meant he was far from healthy. Cash told one reporter at the time: 'I don't think I am a new person. I still sing "A Boy Named Sue" and "Folsom Prison Blues".' But Johnny did pray for a new lease of life so he could overcome his latest illness. A few months later he got a clean bill of health. Now, for the first time in a long while, Johnny Cash had every reason to be happy: a new record label, a stable family, a positive medical assessment and yet another resurgence in popularity. PolyGram Records, ready to promote their 'new' star, planned a round of publicity and promotional trips.

Cash continued broadening his crossover appeal by playing such venues as New York's The Ritz and appearing on the popular *Today Show*. *People* magazine reviewed the Man In Black's latest album and called it 'a never-a-dull-moment project if ever there was one'.

In 1988, the Country Music Hall of Fame honoured Cash with one of the largest exhibitions ever constructed for an entertainer. The organisation also planned a ten-city television and radio circuit to promote tourists to the facility, with all print and billboard ads for the Hall of Fame specifically designed to target the new Cash exhibit. The man himself acted as the curator for the display, which was divided up into seven sections, each representing an historic or cultural phase of Cash's life, including his beginnings, his rise to international stardom and his sense of religious mission. The exhibit is still standing to this day.

As fate would have it, Johnny's extraordinary run of ill health took yet another turn for the worse. In December, 1988, he'd just been in hospital visiting fellow country star Waylon Jennings, who was recovering from bypass surgery, when he was rushed back to the same Nashville hospital suffering from severe chest pains and underwent the same operation as Jennings. To make matters worse, Cash developed a mysterious respiratory disease, which complicated his recovery from the original surgery. Beside him throughout his ordeal was June Carter, who slept in the Baptist Hospital every night. Johnny took more than three weeks to recover from surgery that usually only needs seven days.

Doctors warned Cash he would have once again to change his eating habits and begin a strict exercise programme if he wanted to avoid another – possibly deadly – blood vessel blockage like the one that had made his bypass surgery necessary in the first place. Most worrying of all, strong painkillers were prescribed, as was the case with all such operations. Johnny knew those chemicals could spell disaster for him. He knew only too well he was capable of becoming addicted to any tablets.

On release from hospital, Johnny Cash immediately and sensibly checked himself voluntarily into the Betty Ford Center, for the second time, telling newsmen with blunt honesty: 'I came in sober and I came in straight. Anyone who has undergone drug treatment has the chance of a relapse, and I am wise enough to know it. I enjoy my life too much to do that.'

Doctors informed Johnny of something he'd feared all along: any medication could potentially spark off his drug addiction problems all over again. He was going to have to take corrective treatment after every visit he ever made to a hospital for the rest of his life. But Cash considered it a very small price to pay for staying off those dreaded pills.

Further talk of drug problems surfaced following some botched dental work, which resulted in Johnny's jaw being broken. Somewhere along the line, infection set in and he was in excruciating pain. The singer turned to Percodan to relieve the pain and started taking twenty pills a day, though he quickly reduced his intake and just about managed to stop himself becoming addicted.

• • • •

The one character trait that most people reckoned still made Johnny Cash such a loved individual was his honesty. He had never tried to hide his addiction to pills and, beforehand, booze. He had always spoken his mind with remarkable frankness and often even let his songs do his talking for him. With guitar perched on his lap, Johnny Cash offered the story of his personal battle against chemical dependency to a drug and alcohol abuse conference in Fayetteville, in the summer of 1989. 'I'm here today sober and grateful to God for the wonderful life he has given me,' Johnny told an audience of about three hundred counsellors and recovering alcoholics and drug addicts. 'I've lived nine lives. I really have.'

Johnny then proceeded to sing, speak, play his guitar and answer questions from the audience during a one-and-a-half-hour appearance. When it was all over, the crowd gave him a standing ovation and Fayetteville City Director Mike Green presented Johnny with the key to the city. It was a personal triumph for the singer – he'd managed to turn the misery and suffering of all those previous years into a story to inspire millions who might have problems with similar demons.

In the summer of 1990, Johnny proved his loyalty to one of his oldest and closest friends in the music industry by bailing out Roy Orbison's down-and-out son. The singer heard that Wesley Orbison, 26, was struggling to live after a series of tragedies including the death of his mother in a motorbike accident, followed harrowingly by his brothers' death in a fire at their house next door to Johnny's place on Old Hickory Lake and finally his father's death in 1988. Cash stepped in and gave Wesley a valuable piece of real estate next to his home which he'd bought off Roy Orbison twenty years earlier. 'Use it any way you want,' Johnny told Orbison's son. 'Your daddy would have wanted you to have it.'

At the beginning of the 1990s, Johnny Cash made a conscious effort to ease off and enjoy his life more on a personal level. He even considered selling his beloved house on the edge of Old Hickory Lake after enduring years of busloads of tourists gawping at him most mornings. But, in the end, he decided the house was so important to his family that to sell it would mark a parting of the ways of all those closest to him. All around the house there were reminders of Johnny, June and the children, including John Carter's footprints in the concrete outside the back door from when he had been brought home as a newborn baby. His daughter Rosanne had been married at the house amid a glamorous gathering of celebrities. By this time, Johnny and June already had sixteen grandchildren. Cash cut back from over one hundred concerts a year to around the fifty mark and he steadfastly refused to ever work on a Sunday.

Out in Hollywood, he continued to make acting appearances, including a recreation of the John Wayne role in *Three Godfathers*, and also wrote a movie script. Cash told his family and friends he'd never retire. He would, he promised, continue to write songs until the day he dropped. As part of a new fitness regimen, he embarked upon a diet that helped him trim twenty pounds and started regularly working out in his private gym, as well as walking two miles every day.

In 1991, Johnny once again demonstrated his affection for the armed forces when he performed a song written by an air force sergeant serving in the Middle East as part of Operation Desert Shield. Sgt Jeffrey Grantham, a 30-year-old aspiring songwriter from Kokomo, Ind., had sent his tune 'A Love Song to America' to Ralph Emery, host of TV show *Nashville Now*. The show's producers were so impressed they passed the song on to Cash. He jumped at the opportunity to honour American troops and performed the patriotic song on national cable TV.

• • • •

Las Vegas had long represented a pot of gold at the end of the rainbow for many legendary singing stars such as Frank Sinatra, Wayne Newton, Dolly Parton and many more. Nashville served the same purpose for Johnny Cash and various other country stars. But in the early 1990s, a new giant location emerged that was ready to take on the big boys and pay handsomely for the privilege. The once-quiet farming town of Branson, Missouri, located 30 miles south of Springfield, was predominantly a business district with a long strip called Highway 76 running right through it. Developers decided to create a sort of Las Vegas/Nashville to attract tourist business to the region. It took off much more quickly than anyone had expected and several country music stars, including Roy Clark, Boxcar Willie and Mel Tillis, had soon built entertainment complexes in the area, by simply donating their name and making an occasional appearance. Silver Dollar City, a mammoth theme park was converted into Dollywood, a Dolly Parton 'theme park', and attendance went through the roof.

In 1991, Johnny Cash got a call from the people at Branson asking if he'd be interested in the idea of helping create 'Cash Country', a $35 million entertainment complex located on more than 80 acres of land. It was to include three music theatres, a horse arena, a go-kart track, a water park and an auction house. In the music theatres, gospel, country and other types of music would be featured with Johnny becoming one of the park's regular entertainers. There were also plans for a second stage to include a hotel with more than 350 rooms, three smaller motels and a 20,000 sq ft shopping mall. Cash pledged to participate. 'Johnny says this will totally reorganise his schedule, that he plans to spend a lot of time out there,' said one record company rep.

Developers claimed that Cash Country would also provide 300 full-time jobs, 450 seasonal jobs and an annual payroll of $6 million to $7 million. Devoted fans seemed enthralled by the prospect of a permanent home for their number-one star. Billboards with Johnny's picture stated 'Come see the Johnny Cash Theater'. But it was not to be. When the fans started turning up a year or so later – in November 1992 – all they found was a cinder block shell. The developers of the park had declared bankruptcy even though fans of the superstar singer had put down a whopping $250,000 for advance tickets and Johnny himself later claimed he lost $2.5 million in fees that had been promised to him from the outset.

The curse of addiction that had plagued Cash and his family for so long struck again in the early 1990s, when his only son John Carter was admitted to the Cumberland Heights Drug and Alcohol Treatment Center, in Nashville. His problem was booze and the family insisted he was nipping his problems in the bud before they took over and ruined his life the way they had for his father. John Carter had earlier told his mother and father he blamed his drink problems on his family and had stormed out of a meeting with his parents at the mansion near Hendersonville. The 21-year-old had stayed away from his family for weeks, but finally returned and agreed to be admitted for treatment.

The news about John Carter sparked the beginning of even more drink- and drug-related problems – this time facing four of June and Johnny's daughters: Cindy, Rosey, Tara and Rosanne. It seemed that Johnny's demons were threatening the stability and happiness of his family, not just him. Cash called on his old friend, evangelist Billy Graham, to help guide him through this devastating family crisis. The two men had been friends for more than twenty years and Graham gave Johnny a special 24-hour phone number for him to call any time for advice. Eventually, Billy Graham ended up counselling Johnny at least twice a day by phone and he encouraged the singer to turn to God even more, to control his pain and anger. Billy Graham convinced Johnny Cash the worst was now over and he should get on with his life. But Johnny couldn't help asking himself how much more of this could happen. And was it all his fault?

19

'THE COOLEST MAN
IN THE WORLD'

Johnny Cash had now become something of an elder
statesman in the music industry. He'd long since come into
his own, although essentially he was doing nothing that
different from the way he'd been performing for the previous
forty years. Johnny was the same singer doing the same
professional job. He had aged, even mellowed a bit, perhaps
grown wiser and more secure, but he didn't suddenly become
a different person or a greater performer overnight.

But Cash was aware that he was now being seen as one
of the most significant contributors to the music scene in
modern times. His strengths were now even more obvious,
as was his ability to shrug off indifferent songs that any
performer of his stature seemed to be forced to take on from
time to time. There are those performers who achieve
hipness and then there are those who transcend that fleeting

state and become, simply, *cool*. Johnny Cash had most definitely become the latter, as he found out in 1992 when he was inducted into The Rock And Roll Hall Of Fame, joining The Rolling Stones, The Who, Elvis Presley and Roy Orbison. 'Johnny Cash is the coolest man in the world,' gushed Emmylou Harris at the ceremony. 'I think they invented the word "charisma" to describe what Johnny Cash has.' Rock'n'roll icon Bono of U2 insisted: 'I would rather spend the day with Johnny Cash than a week with any up-and-coming pop star.' US rock legend Bruce Springsteen admitted he'd listened to Cash's early Sun Recordings when working on his album *Nebraska*. And the tributes flowed on.

Now the Man in Black was being feted by those who seemed to be more attracted to his dark side, his moodiness, his unavailability. All the things that made him so fearsome when he was fighting those demons were now the ultimate calling card. Cash took all the adoration with a characteristic grain of salt. Everything was summed up for him at the Hall of Fame ceremony when he found himself at a urinal as Keith Richards walked in, stood behind him and started singing 'Loading Coal' from Johnny's *Ride This Train* album. Then he added, 'Look at this. I'm taking a piss with Johnny Cash. We need a picture of this!' Johnny insisted to the Rolling Stone, 'No, Keith, we don't need a picture of this.'

His glory days of mammoth record sales might have passed, but Cash's good work continued. His album *The Mystery of Life* was released in 1990 to universal praise from the critics, although it sold in relatively small quantities. Of course, by this stage in his career Johnny Cash's significance could no longer be measured merely by record sales. For decades now he had been one of the most famous men in the country. During one trip to Branson, Missouri, the Man in Black went to the local Wal-Mart supermarket to do some last-minute shopping before a European tour by The Highwaymen. Pushing a cart through the men's clothing department, Johnny was instantly recognised by virtually everyone who saw him. But Cash simply couldn't be bothered to try and disguise himself. He had done that a few years earlier when he put on a blond wig and some sunglasses and a yellow shirt – and ended up looking like Johnny Cash in a disguise. The first person he ran into said, 'Hi, Johnny.' Cash shrugged his shoulders, signed an autograph and carried on with his shopping.

The year 1992 also saw yet another mini-explosion in interest in country music on a much broader spectrum, although Cash would insist it had been been big for the previous thirty years. Cash believed his hard work in Nashville in the 1960s had initiated the original explosion in interest and that had never fallen away. But, with more and more rock'n'roll performers paying homage to Johnny Cash, it was making him a very fashionable figure in the industry yet again.

In a *Rolling Stone* interview in December, 1992, Johnny's legendary status was confirmed by the nature of the journalist's questions, which included requests for Johnny's views on politics, Elvis Presley, Richard Nixon, Martin Luther King, Robert Kennedy and Booker T Washington. It was certainly all a far cry from 'What does "A Boy Named Sue" really mean?' When Johnny was asked whether he thought what was happening in 1992 would be good for country music in the long run, he had an interesting answer:

> *I think so, 'cause there's so many people striking out in so many different directions. But only the best will prevail. Who knows whether Garth Brooks has got any staying power? I feel some have staying power, but a big group of them need to be sure they can get their day job back. The trouble is, Nashville is crazy for jumping on trends. For every good artist there are ten clones trying to sound like that one artist. Here I am sounding like I'm blowing my horn, but I wanna see somebody strike out in a different direction as Johnny Cash did in 1955. I haven't heard anything like that in Nashville since Kris Kristofferson.*

It was an intriguing response because obviously Johnny believed that many of the new stars did not have the staying power – and as the Nineties progressed he was to be proved absolutely correct. During this period, Johnny became involved in a TV programme that many of his fans had definitely never bothered to watch – *Sesame Street*. The star, now past his sixtieth birthday, began making regular appearances after the show introduced a new character called Ronnie Trash, who dressed in black and cleared up trash everywhere he went. Johnny later admitted he could relate to that character!

One of the sadder aspects of Johnny Cash's so-called 'reinvention' as a trendy performer was that he took it upon himself to pledge never to sing 'A Boy Named Sue' again. He'd actually grown to hate the song; it was no longer funny to him. He'd heard it so much he was sick of every word of it. Cash just prayed that his adoring public would let him forget it. Of course, they wouldn't and many felt disappointed at his decision.

Johnny's rock'n'roll status moved up yet another notch when, in 1993, U2's Bono asked the Man in Black to sing the lead vocals on 'The Wanderer', the closing track on the band's smash hit album *Zooropa*. As *Interview* magazine commented: 'Cash isn't becoming hip again; he's just reminding us how hip he's always been.' U2's Bono admitted that what attracted him to Cash was his ability to seem dangerous. 'I mean, it's not just the voice and the spirit. There's something unnerving about the way he sings. I felt Elvis, like everyone else, just took bits and pieces from everyone around him. He had Valentino's haircut, Roy Orbison's voice at the end of his range, and Dean Martin's at the bottom. But Elvis would have been a sissy if he hadn't met Johnny Cash.' Johnny himself admitted his involvement with U2 would probably surprise a few fans, but insisted: 'It's not some far-out kind of wedding. I was very comfortable working with U2. I've known them several years. Bono is brilliant, he knows all about country and rockabilly.'

In December, 1993, Cash made an uncharacteristic, unannounced appearance at Johnny Depp's Viper Rooms club, on Sunset Boulevard, West Hollywood. His guest-list-only gig at the venue – now infamous as the place where young actor River Phoenix died of a drugs overdose – attracted a reverent full house of celebs, including Sean Penn, Juliette Lewis, Patricia Arquette, Flea from Red Hot Chili Peppers, Henry Rollins and Butthead Surfers frontman Gibby Haynes.

Johnny Cash genuinely believed that mixing with young musicians and actors could prove more inspirational than anything he had done in years. He later recalled: 'I thought, why not? Young people especially see so much video and film that they know what's real when they see it. They appreciate the honest and open barin' of emotions. And you can't have any more honesty than just takin' a guitar up there and singin' your songs.' The Man in Black – almost three times the age of many of his latest followers – also insisted: 'I no longer have a grandiose attitude about my music being a powerful force for change. I think today's youth sees the hypocrisy in government, the rotten core of social ills and poverty and prejudice, and I'm not afraid to say that's where the trouble is.'

• • • •

Johnny Cash remained most at home with the simple things in life. Sure, he was a wanderer and a lone ranger, but then it was those characteristics which had helped him drag country music into a place in modern music. Johnny helped fuel the American myth: his songs were tributes to the impossibility of freedom.

In his early sixties, he decided to reinvent himself again and signed a new record deal with the decidedly unconservative

Def American label, to produce a freshly made package for a modern musical era. Some believed it had something to do with the resurgence of such old timers as Frank Sinatra and Tony Bennett although the hype surrounding these two legends seemed more like a frantic dance around two creaking wax figures. Yet Johnny Cash emerged fresh and ready for battle, even more dangerous and infinitely more alive. He signed with a new producer, Rick Rubin, who'd previously worked with artists such as The Beastie Boys on his Def Jam label and The Black Crowes and rapper Sir Mix-a-Lot on Def American. The hairy studio virtuoso who favoured ripped jeans and the Man in Black seemed an unlikely team at the outset.

Cash's first venture with his new label was titled *American Recordings* and established the Man in Black as 'the godfather of gloom' for the Nineties. According to a *New York Times* review of the album, the intention seemed to be to reveal 'that his tales of darkness and doubt are not dead ends, but thoroughfares in the struggle that is life.' The first single to be released, named 'Delia's Gone', was actually recorded several years before by Cash. The song pulled no punches. Cash portrayed a lover, enraged by his girlfriend's infidelity – retribution comes in the form of shotgun blasts to her chest as she is tied to a chair.

The video for the song, featuring supermodel Kate Moss as Cash's dead girlfriend, was rejected by MTV, who did not approve of the graphic portrayal of Delia's burial. Johnny became the only man alive with the distinction of having a music video rejected by MTV because of violence and purported bad taste while at the same time being a regular speaker at Billy Graham crusades!

Johnny Cash believed he'd hit a point where he was just spinning his wheels and not actually accomplishing anything new or special. Nashville was doing all right without him and now he had to do all right without Nashville. But time hadn't mellowed him. It had just caused his split-level nature to develop into separate personas – both of which Cash had become very comfortable with.

On the live concert front, the Man in Black was still managing to pack in the crowds. His shows were usually filled with rolling applause, a sound like combers rushing in; shrieks, catcalls, cowpoke hoots, pigeon yee-hoos, all before he'd even walked on the stage. Behind the scenes, Cash would forever be restlessly prowling along a corridor like a circuit riding preacher who sensed the imminence of hellfire. His nostrils flared. He'd finally stride down the hall, clasping his hands together and tensing them forward over his head, tensing and exercising his shoulders and neck. His head held back. He was aloof, stern, withholding. Onstage, the songs came fast and furious. In the audience, a faded cotton crewcut procession of mild-mannered folk, both young and old. These were the 1990s fans of Johnny Cash.

By his mid-sixties Johnny Cash had become the sort of hard-bitten desperado that even a fifteen-year-old heavy metal fan could adore. Posed sternly between the hounds of hell on the cover of *American Recordings*, Johnny Cash looked menacing and deadly. He'd devised the cover himself and even nicknamed the featured dogs 'Sin' and 'Redemption'. The production of the album was high concept and low tech. Much of the taping was done at Johnny's cabin in the grounds of his mansion near

Hendersonville, and in the living room of Rick Rubin's Los Angeles home.

Interestingly, Rubin did not try to push Cash on to a commercial bandwagon. Instead, he helped capture the rich essence of the singer-songwriter better than any recordings since the first Folsom Prison album back in the early 1960s. Cash consciously decided that the songs that ended up on the album should be about the theme of sin and redemption. Cash saw it as a vivid picture of the dark and glorious in life.

Johnny was aiming at another generation. The album was well received, but it seemed doubtful whether its sales would ever approach the dizzy heights of its many predecessors. Just after Cash had completed recording that new album, the young rock star Kurt Cobain committed suicide. Johnny read about the tragedy with great interest because he knew that Cobain meant so much to his followers; in a way, his impact had been similar to the effect that Johnny Cash had had in his early days. 'Everybody likes to hear something they can identify with,' Cash argued, 'and we can see that millions of young people identified with Cobain's music. That's what music is about: communication. It doesn't matter if it's country or blues or rock. The most important music comes from the gut ... It's something that is honest.'

Johnny Cash knew all about the pressures of stardom. He'd found it all incredibly hard to cope with. How it took over his life. How it changed everything and everyone around him. That was why drugs came into his life and took over for so many years. Cash knew he couldn't handle the success. But then a lot of other people couldn't either. He later recalled: 'In the early years, it was like I felt guilty about it all. I had come from this real poor background and I didn't feel like I deserved all this money and attention. I kept thinking, I'm not what they think I am. I don't have all the answers. I'm not magic. But then you grow with it, and you learn that it really doesn't matter what other people think of you. You're just one human being and you're doing the best you can. But it's not easy. It almost destroyed me. There but for the grace of God ... you know the line.'

In 1994 Johnny Cash had an experience that perfectly summed up how he'd turned his life around. He walked out on to the boat dock of his mansion in Hendersonville and found himself face to face with a four-foot snake. One more step and he would have stepped right on it. He gently pushed his fishing pole in the direction of the snake and coaxed him back into the water. The old Johnny Cash would have killed that snake in a split second.

In the grounds of his beloved house, Cash had carefully nurtured a nature reserve – some would call it a zoo – that now consisted of a goofy llama, Zelda the goose, a peacock and 33 deer. There had been an ostrich too, but that had had to go after it had attacked Johnny a few years back. He'd even had two bison, but they banged up the air-conditioning unit and nearly ran over some of Johnny's friends and family, so they'd been shipped out.

But then the 150 acres that surrounded the house on Old Hickory Lake was more than just peace and solitude to Johnny Cash. He believed that the land had been ordained by God and he dedicated it all to Him. One day he'd been poking around with a metal detector and dug up an old Civil War-era branding iron forged with the initials JC. In Cash's complex mind, that represented the conflicting forces of sin and redemption. Simple elements mixed with complex emotional issues had now taken on much more significance in his life. Sometimes when he fished, Johnny Cash thought about singing. 'And sometimes when I'm performin',' he later recalled. 'I'm thinkin' about my fishin' pole.'

But men like Johnny Cash didn't fish for too long.

• • • •

In the mid-1990s, a young British journalist called Pete Clark met Johnny Cash at a concert in Helsinki, Finland, where he was playing with The Highwaymen. Half an hour before the show, Clark received a message saying that Cash had nothing to do and that they could meet for a chat backstage. A golden opportunity for a young writer, but one that Clark found himself incapable of rising to. As he later recalled: 'The Man in Black completely unnerved me, and I sat looking at him unable to come up with anything to say, other than the fact it was snowing outside. He gave me a cool look. "I'm not getting anything out of this, and neither are you. Get out of here, kid." It may not have been my best interview, but I remember it fondly. After all, the man is a legend.'

Cash's style, which had seemed to be almost trendy in the early 1990s, once again fell victim to fashion. His sparse delivery was deemed too uncompromising for many modern palates. But Cash's fighting qualities remained undiminished. In 1994, he made an appearance at the Glastonbury Rock Festival, deep in the heart of the English countryside. Accompanied by an acoustic guitar he sang about sin and redemption and brought tears to everyone's eyes. One critic later said his performances were so deeply felt, so right, that a law should have been passed to make everyone listen to them.

In 1995, Cash had to cancel another British tour because of nerve damage in his face. It was later identified as a form of Parkinson's disease called Shy-Drager syndrome, which rapidly turned his black hair completely white. Within eighteen months, sickness was wracking that once strong body and those who saw him talked about vast weight loss and a puffy face that was sagging and startling to the eye. Finally, it seemed, the Man in Black was starting to fade.

20

END OF THE LINE

Through the last couple of years of the 1990s, Johnny Cash's health began to deteriorate. First came another disease of the nervous system, called autonomic neuropathy, followed by severe bouts of pneumonia. Cash told one close friend: 'When you know death is in town you should quit gazin' out the windows at the lake and start tellin' your stories.' By this time, Cash's once huge frame was wasted by the incessant bouts of pneumonia he described as 'like bein' kicked in the lungs every minute by two massive horses'.

By 2000 Cash's medical bills were so large he had to sell some of his property, including the House of Cash museum on the Nashville street they named after him, Johnny Cash Parkway. Yet despite his illnesses, he continued to give live performances and even occasionally appeared on television talk shows. In London, Cash gave a one-off live show and was so annoyed by a sore throat, which ruined the last half of his performance, that he came back to the microphone and told the audience he was going to do it all over again. As music critic Gavin Martin later recalled: 'And he did, it's not something I'd ever seen before, nor something I ever expect to see again."

As if sensing that time was short, Cash himself was now increasingly prone to reflections on his career and musicianship. He told one interviewer: 'When I write, it's a special thing. I don't write songs just to have something to sing for the wind. I get up in the morning singing and thinking about music. I play the guitar and listen to records. No matter what I'm doing, I'm humming or keeping time with my fingers to a beat going on in my head. If I couldn't sing a song or listen to music I think I'd go crazy.' Cash ended the interview with a classic piece of advice for any up-and-coming musicians: 'Don't sleep with your whisky bottle by the bed. That's a piece of advice that has probably kept me alive this long."

In the early 2000s, Cash also continued recording with Rick Rubin, who helped produce three more albums including *American IV: The Man Comes Around*, which hit the album charts in early 2002. Johnny later insisted the title track had been inspired by the Queen of England: 'I dreamed I was in Buckingham Palace one time and the Queen said to me, "Johnny Cash, you're just like a thorn tree in a whirlwind."'

But the pain his illnesses were causing him was taking its toll. Wife June remained an ever-present force by his side, but those close to the family said she was finding Cash's problems a great strain on her own health. In May, 2003, and now aged 73, June went into hospital for what the family presumed would be a routine heart operation. But she died after surgery, leaving Johnny Cash devastated and all alone for the first time in his life. As one moving obituary in London's *Daily Telegraph* pointed out: 'The two made a contrasting pair: she demure in manner and dress; he foulmouthed and argumentative, even on stage.'

A few weeks after June's death – at the MTV Video Music Awards, in August, 2003 – Johnny Cash received seven nominations for his cover version of the heavy-rock group Nine Inch Nails song 'Hurt'. The Man in Black was too sick to attend. But newly crowned pop heartthrob Justin Timberlake – who'd beaten him to the Best Male Video award – waved the trophy and recalled: 'My grandfather raised me on Johnny Cash. I'm from Tennessee so I guess I share this with him in some cool way.'

Following June's death, Johnny Cash turned his computer website into a moving tribute to his departed wife. He said: 'She was my wife, lover, friend, my biggest critic.' He even started work on a tribute album to her – songs written specifically to help him cope with her death. But the pain etched on his face whenever he mentioned June's name was clear to all around him. Cash was videotaped by close family members singing at the family home in Tennessee. Burl Boykin, a promoter and friend from Oxford, Mississippi, later recalled: 'I don't think that video could ever be released publicly. It was very sad. He couldn't hold his guitar pick or anything. He just cried.'

In early September, 2003, Cash's diabetes took a turn for the worse. Then in the early hours of September 11, he was rushed to the Baptist Hospital, in Nashville, with stomach pains. It was a place he'd grown accustomed to after many years of dicing with death. The staff were almost like a second family to the great man. But this time his maker had called and at 7:00am that morning Johnny Cash died from respiratory failure. The 71-year-old's health had plunged following June's death. Many of his family and friends were convinced he had died from a broken heart.

The Man in Black went to his final resting place on Monday, September 15, 2003, following a star-studded funeral near Nashville. Former US Vice-President Al Gore, and the singers Sheryl Crow and Emmylou Harris were among those paying tributes to the man Kris Kristofferson described that afternoon as 'Abraham Lincoln with a wild side.'

June's passing had been the final hammer blow from which Johnny Cash could never recover. She'd helped him overcome drug addiction and countless other demons to rule the world of country music. The Man in Black could not go on alone.

EPILOGUE

'Success,' Johnny Cash once said, 'is having to worry about every damn thing in the world except money. I still don't understand it. If you don't have time for yourself, any time to hunt or fish, that's success?'

Johnny Cash never knew what lay in store for him, but he did know there were things that he still wanted to do that even he would never achieve. He might not have known what they were, but he felt certain they existed. It was almost like when he was seventeen years old and his mother heard him singing for the first time after his voice had dropped. At the time she'd said: 'God's hand is on you, you're going to be a well-known singer.' Johnny had smiled at her and said simply, 'Oh, Momma' in reply. But he knew she was right. Back then, the big deal was singing on the radio – and when he was just seventeen years old he knew he'd be singing on the radio. He also knew that people would soon know his name. So, there were still things for him to do, even when the end finally came. The books, the TV shows, the movies – none of them were *it*. Johnny Cash never knew what was meant for him.

As his brother Tommy once put it, 'Johnny's as complex as anything God or man put on this earth. He's a man of uncommon characteristics, mentally and physically. Even though you're his brother, or his wife, or his mother, you never know him completely. I've felt myself at times trembling because of my inadequacy around him. And then there's the times I feel completely at ease.'

The face may have been more scarred and craggy than a strip-mined Appalachian mountainside. His deep, rumbling voice may well have preferred to converse with God or the dogwoods than anybody else. The long silences and faraway glances between words became ever longer. The simple country boy never really grew up. As his friend Kris Kristofferson noted: 'He's a walking contradiction, partly truth and partly fiction.'

Johnny Cash was steeped in the lore of black gospel music, folk music, hillbilly laments, the songs of prison cells and chain gangs. His music could be uplifting and inspirational, but at the same time he wasn't afraid to confront his, and our, blacker inclinations. 'He had an incredibly dark side,' recalled his daughter Rosanne, herself known for turning pain into song. 'A lot of it was created from the grief in his life, and of course it's part of what made his art so compelling.'

That art brought a fifty-year career that yielded more than fifty hit singles, seven Grammy Awards, over fifty million album sales, and countless inductions into the Country Music and Rock and Roll Halls of Fame. The message and the sermon in his songs were in his flesh. He was, in Bob Dylan's words, a 'sad-eyed prophet' for a literal Christianity of fundamentalist belief and constant re-enactment, a belief that was slowly dying throughout small-town America, but not among old-time Johnny Cash fans. He'd put himself under sentence of death for them and they revered him for it – even when the end finally came.

Walking taller than John Wayne in elevator boots, Johnny Cash remains the finest example of the mythological American Man. A lot of stars sell millions of records by draping themselves in the mantle of the outlaw, but no one ever combined the messages of piety and violence as Cash did for almost fifty years. He didn't mellow with age. If anything, he grew less sentimental by the day. Famed for his humanitarianism, Johnny was nonetheless drawn to darkness like an anti-moth. Freed from his pill-popping blues, the clean, clear-headed Johnny Cash was still a man in turmoil with himself until the end finally dawned.

So it must have been a relief when out of that darkness came the light ...

ACKNOWLEDGEMENTS

Thanks and much gratitude to John Blake, Adam Parfitt and the rest of the team at John Blake Publishing for making this book possible. Special words also to Mark Sandelson for providing the perfect location for the peace and solitude required to complete this book.

Deepest appreciation to Elizabeth Browning, John Smith, John Glatt, Joe Paolella, Geoff Garvey, plus all the close friends and associates of Johnny Cash who've made invaluable contributions to this book. I fully appreciate their insistence on remaining anonymous.

Books that have proved invaluable include *The Man in Black* by Johnny Cash (Warner Books, 1975); *A Boy Named Cash* by Albert Govini (Lancer Books, 1970); *From the Heart* by June Carter Cash (Prentice Hall Press, 1987);

Winners Got Scars Too – The Life and Legends of Johnny Cash by Christopher S Wren (The Dial Press, 1971).

Finally, most thanks to Johnny Cash for providing an incredible life story to reveal to the world.